Handcrafted Handbags

Book 3

LEISURE ARTS, INC. • Maumelle, Arkansas

Meet the *Designer*

AMANDA SALADIN

I've been designing knit and crochet patterns since 2011, but my love of design goes back much farther than that.

I received a BS in Apparel Design from Middle Tennessee State University in 2002 and have been crafty my whole life. Once I discovered the joys of knitting and crocheting I have never looked back.

I share free knit and crochet patterns for the whole family at ***lovelifeyarn.com*** and have more than 70 published patterns. When I'm not playing with yarn, you can find me hanging out in our home near Nashville, TN with my four boys, my husband of 16 years and my menagerie of animals.

contents

intermediate patterns

Introduction

I love bags. As a designer, I find myself drawn to certain types of projects again and again. There is something about a well-made handbag that really speaks to me. For a handbag to look professional, there is a lot that goes on behind the scenes. It's not just about the crochet, although that is the start of it all.

Behind every great crocheted handbag is a lot of work and dedication. There are the hours spend lovingly creating the crocheted pieces, followed by the application of firm stabilizer to hold its shape, hardware and zippers installed, and a lining fabric carefully stitched and attached. The magic is in the details.

For some, this may seem like an insurmountable obstacle – all the extra things that may or may not already be in the skill set. That's why I wanted to write this series. To take the steps needed to create a designer-quality handbag and break them down so that anyone could understand. It's not that hard, but most of the battle is simply knowing how to do it.

Good finishing is just as important as good crochet. Without it, your bags will never look like you purchased them at a boutique. How do you accomplish good finishing? It takes a few basic skills and planning, but this all can be learned and applied. Making your own bags does not have to be difficult or tedious or take forever. I know we all have limited time!

So today, the curtain is pulled back and the mystery of a high quality, homemade handbag is revealed. I want to walk you through every step in creating a handbag you will be proud to carry. I have a very specific process that I use when I create handbags, and every bag in this book was created using it. I love it when I get asked where I got my bag and I can proudly say "I made it myself!". I want you to feel that way, too. And, with a little hard work and some help from this book – you can. I'm here to guide you every step of the way. Now the hardest part will be figuring out what you want to make first!

I hope this series inspires you to try something new and to develop a love of handcrafted handbags.

HOW TO USE THIS BOOK

This book is intended to be a reference of all the skills needed to create quality crocheted handbags. I recommend starting with some of the smaller or simpler projects to become familiar with the basic techniques and moving on to more complex bags as you become more confident in your skills. However the projects in this book are rated Intermediate.

INTERMEDIATE *Intermediate*

These projects assume that one can follow instructions, read basic crochet abbreviations, stitch accurately, and understanding how a bag is constructed. These projects are a little more detailed and will take a bit longer to complete. They also include more difficult crochet stitches, such as cables.

You will see that there are basic finishing instructions for each pattern. For help with a particular skill, reference the section in the book that goes into detail for that skill. It would be helpful to read over the sections for each skill before jumping in to the finishing section of a bag. As you become familiar with the basic construction techniques, you will find you no longer need to reference these sections as frequently. Eventually, you may not need them at all, and that is the whole goal of this book – to take you to a point of confidence in your ability to create designer-quality handbags of your own.

CHAPTER 1 Handbag *Basics*

Before getting into the technical details of linings, interfacings, and hardware, let's take a few minutes and look at some basics of handbag construction. We will learn how to choose projects wisely, how to swatch for success and the anatomy of a handbag. The next chapter we will delve into the materials you will need and how to choose the best yarn for your project.

CHOOSING A PROJECT

Before you begin, it's important to carefully choose your project. Take time to read over the pattern and see what techniques are used. Review the materials list and what items are used in the finishing of the bag. Does this pattern call for interfacing? Lining? What type of yarn does that pattern call for? All of these, and more, are important questions to ask when choosing a pattern.

Most patterns that I have seen for crocheted handbags do not use any kind of lining or stabilizer, giving it a floppy shape and less-than-ideal finishing. To be truly useful, most crocheted bags need some form of supportive infrastructure. Market bags and bags with an open, lacy stitch are notable exceptions to this rule.

So what if you want to add these things to an existing handbag pattern? You easily can, using the techniques in this book, but be sure to really read over the project instructions before you begin. If the pattern is too open, the stabilizer will show through. These types of projects take a lot of careful planning and consideration, but in the end, you will be glad you took the time before you started work.

There are things you should look for to help you decide if the project will be successful or if you should keep looking. These are:

PATTERN INSTRUCTIONS

Always read through a pattern completely before deciding if it is an appropriate project. You want a pattern with clear, well-written instructions. Make sure you understand all the directions, abbreviations, and special stitches. Also, be sure you understand the construction of the bag. How is it put together? If you are adding stabilizer and lining not in the pattern, how difficult will it be to redo the finishing instructions to accommodate this?

SIZE

The preferred size of a handbag varies considerably. How big is this bag you are making? Will it be too big or too small for your liking? The best way I have found to answer this question is to get out a bag you already own that is a size you like. Take detailed measurements of this bag and compare it to the project you are considering. How does it compare? For me, I like larger totes as I have several smaller children, so I wouldn't want to commit to a project and start working, only to find that it is simply too small and having to abandon the project.

YARN

Consider the type of yarn used in the design. Is this pattern calling for a specific type of yarn, such as mohair or t-shirt yarn? What will happen if you substitute the yarn called for in the pattern? You may like the yarn used in the pattern and go with it. Personally, if I am making a high end handbag, I am going to go with a natural fiber or blend. I have found in my experience that these give the best results.

After you have studied the pattern and considered these items, you may decide whether to move forward with this pattern or continue your search. Don't settle for anything less than what you really want. It's not worth putting all the time and effort into a bag if the desired result is not to your liking. Keep looking until you find the right pattern.

SUCCESSFUL SWATCHING

Before beginning any project where size matters, you must swatch. I know, I know, I hate to swatch when I am eager to begin a project! But, I have learned it is of the utmost importance when you are trying to make a piece to a certain size. Even just half a stitch off from the gauge can give you a dramatically different result. Learn to love swatching.

I used to do the absolute smallest swatch I could get away with. Most of them I could only measure a 2" x 2" (5 cm x 5 cm) square. That's really much too small to give you any real information, and I often found as I worked my pattern pieces that the gauge differed from my tiny swatch. Sometimes, I wouldn't catch this until much later, and then I had to start all over. I learned my lesson, and now I swatch before beginning most every project.

This is especially important if you substituted the yarn called for in the pattern. Swatching will give you an idea of how the yarn will work up and if it will have the same characteristics of the original yarn. Can you get the correct gauge with the new yarn? Will you have to go up or down a hook size? These are important questions that need to be answered before beginning any project.

You can also get a much better idea of how much yarn you will need when you swatch. Nothing is worse than almost being done with a project and running out of yarn! This still sometimes happens to me and it is one of the most frustrating things ever. Typically now I will buy at least a skein extra just so this won't happen – and then I have a lot of single skeins laying around! Most stores will take back an unused skein, but I just end up keeping them.

ANATOMY OF A HANDBAG

Before we begin discussing the techniques in detail, let's take a few moments to look at the parts that make up a well-made crochet handbag. Understanding how a handbag is put together and the materials that help it keep its shape will better help you understand how to finish it.

Vintage Handbag instructions available in #7916

THE OUTER CROCHETED SHELL

This is the part that you see on the outside and what we think of when we picture a crocheted handbag. Usually constructed in several parts and seamed together, this is the start of a handcrafted handbag.

THE STABILIZER

If you want a bag to keep its shape, it absolutely has to have a stabilizing layer. I've tried several things over the years but have found that Craft Stabilizer works the best for my designs. It's thick and stiff enough to hold a shape but has enough give that you don't feel like you are carrying a brick. Certain bags, however, can skip the stabilizer if they are meant to have a softer shape.

THE LINING

A functional crocheted bag will have a fabric lining. The lining will help keep the crocheted stitches from stretching out, especially if you make a bag that does not have stabilizer. It looks nicer inside, plus you can add in extra pockets if you want.

THE HANDLES

Most all bags have handles of some sort. If it's a bag that is meant to be carried, handles are a must. You can buy purchased handles made from leather, fabric or other materials, or you can crochet them. If I crochet handles, I like to reinforce them with jute cord or nylon webbing so that they don't stretch out. Bags can have one long strap or two handles, and a few have both options.

THE CLOSURE

A lot of bags will have some type of closure, whether it be a zipper, button, or magnetic snap. This keeps all the belongings securely inside. The type of bag will dictate what type of closure is best.

THE HARDWARE

This includes anything else that might add functionality or a design detail to the bag. Purse feet, grommets, metal rings, etc. These things are useful but not required.

As you can see, there are a lot more things to think about with a crocheted handbag than simply making the pieces. Each of these elements has to be tackled one at a time. If you learn to do them in the right order, you can make any bag your heart desires and make it look professional.

CHAPTER 2 Handbag Maker's *Toolkit*

Having the right tools on hand will make the process of finishing your handbags easier and more enjoyable. Here are some items that are a must in your toolkit.

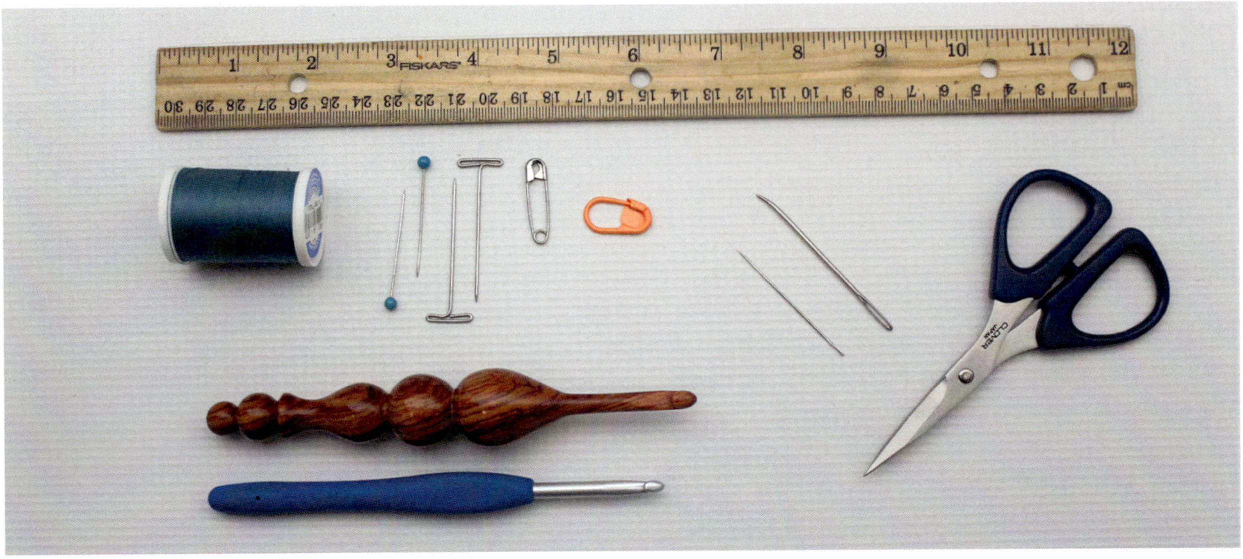

HOOKS

If you have been crocheting for any length of time, you probably have all the hooks you need to make most handbag patterns, except maybe a Tunisian pattern or a larger than usual hook. Since everyone has their own personal preference for the type and style of hook, the hooks you choose to use can be most anything – as long as you can get gauge.

NEEDLES

No, I don't mean knitting needles! You will need a variety of types of needles to create handbags, because the needle that sews your crocheted pieces together is very different from the one you use to attach your lining. Here are the needles I recommend:

Tapestry Needles: These are made for yarn and have a blunt end with a large eye. They are thick and easy to hold. You can find them with either curved or straight tips, and I happen to like them both. You may find that you enjoy using one type over the other. I have many, many tapestry needles because I inevitably end up losing them. Good thing they are inexpensive!

Hand-Sewing Needles: When sewing your linings to your crocheted pieces or attaching the craft stabilizer, you will need to use a sharp hand-sewing needle. You can find these in a variety of sizes and lengths. I prefer one with a bit larger eye (some of the eyes on sewing needles are so small they are difficult to thread) and I like mine to be about an inch and a half long. This is also personal preference, but you will want them to be very sharp and strong enough you don't bend them when sewing (ask me how I know that can happen!).

PINS

You will need pins to help hold your pieces in place as well as to block the pieces. There are three types of pins I use when I am working on a handbag:

T-Pins: I use these for pinning pieces together and for blocking. They do well holding up to getting wet on the blocking board and hold pieces together well.

Ball Head Pins: These are the pins that I use for holding zippers in place and blocking more delicate items. They are a bit thinner than my T-pins and I like the ones with larger heads.

Safety Pins: These can be a life-saver for holding pieces together when regular pins slip out. I use them often to mark placements, hold pieces together and pin buttons in place. Have a variety of sizes on hand – you can pick up a variety pack for cheap at your local discount store.

THREAD

When finishing a handbag, you will need to use quite a bit of thread. I have found that basic hand sewing threads work perfectly. Beware upholstery thread or anything super thick – it does not do as well, especially for applying the lining to your crocheted piece. If you really want an invisible join, they do make clear thread. I used this on a Convertible Clutch (in book #7915) and enjoyed the results, but the thread itself was a bit difficult to use. It is so thin and delicate that you almost can't see where it is, and it tends to curl up on itself a lot. But it does give an invisible result.

SCISSORS

A good pair of sharp scissors is a must. Fabric shears are the best option for this, as you will be cutting craft stabilizer and lining fabrics. Most of the time with crochet, it doesn't really matter what scissors you use as long as they can cut a piece of yarn. To make your life easier, invest in a nice pair of fabric shears that will cut your yarn ends and also glide through a lining fabric.

STITCH MARKERS

When you need to mark a stitch, it will be helpful to have some locking stitch markers on hand. Typically you will mark the first stitch when working in the round, which is where you will find stitch markers listed for use in this book.

RULER

Use a ruler to check your gauge and to measure your finished pieces. You could use a measuring tape, but I have found that measuring tapes can stretch out and throw off your gauge. Now, I use a trusty ruler made of wood, plastic, or metal.

CHOOSING YARN

The yarn you choose will have a major impact on your finished handbag. You will want to consider the colorfastness of the yarn and the way it will wear. If a yarn bleeds or transfers color to another surface, you might find your favorite clothes stained. Take the time up front to check these important items, or you might find later that the yarn you chose was not a good idea.

Let's take a moment to talk about yarn choice. This is really one of the most important parts of your project. Pick the wrong yarn, and the project won't turn out the way you expected it to. You can't expect a cheap acrylic to perform the same way as a superwash wool. No two yarns are the same – in fact, even the same yarn from different dye lots can be very different! I've had this happen before when I ran out of a hand dyed yarn and ordered from a different dye lot. Be sure you have enough yarn to finish the project, and take some time to familiarize yourself with your yarn.

BASIC GUIDELINES FOR CHOOSING A YARN

Always check the ball band and double check the fiber content, weight, and recommended stitch count of a yarn. Check to see the care instructions of the yarn so you can get an idea of how you will be able to clean your bag. You obviously won't want to throw your whole handbag in the wash, so check to see how easy it is to wash the yarn. Some yarns are pretty delicate and might not hold up to a rigorous spot washing. Take time to think about this before you choose a yarn.

Let's look at some fibers that are suitable for handbags:

Wool: Wool is honestly my favorite yarn for handbags. It blocks easily, but beware using heat on it with agitation as it can felt. I like to pin my wool pieces to measurements, then spray with water and allow to dry. Wool works so well for this method.

Cashmere, alpaca, and other animal fibers: These are often found with other yarns in a blend. I tend to really enjoy all animal fibers as there are similar characteristics to wool, although these other animal fibers might not have the same springiness and durability as wool, so I tend to look for them blended with wool, such as in Lion Brand® Yarn's Fifty Fifty yarn.

Silk: I don't tend to use silk yarns much except for small evening projects. The *Puff Stitch Clutch* on page 40 is made from Lion Brand® Hand-Dyed Silk and it was a dream to work with. I also use silk in blends and enjoy this natural fiber. It can take more care, however, so be careful using it for an everyday bag.

Cotton: Another of my favorite fibers, cotton is easy care and easy to work with. It blocks well with water and can accept steaming, if needed. I love cotton for a good summery handbag.

Linen: Another good natural fiber is linen. Linen is strong and durable and will hold up to wear and tear. You will often find linen blended with other fibers. Sometimes 100% linen yarns are stiff, but this can be a good thing with handbags.

Synthetic Yarns: Acrylic, polyester and other synthetic fibers can be used in handbags, but if you are looking for a truly professional-looking handbag, I would recommend a natural fiber, or at least a blend. Synthetic yarns are easy to care for, but be careful applying heat to most of them as the fibers can melt.

SUBSTITUTING YARN

Many times, you will not use the yarn called for in a pattern. When substituting yarn, be sure to use the same weight of yarn (substitute a worsted for a worsted, for example). It is also helpful to try and keep the same fiber content. Look at the yarn symbols on the ball band for information, and try to find yarn with the same wraps per inch (WPI). Always swatch in the new yarn to check gauge.

Once you choose a yarn, take some time to create a swatch to see the characteristics of your chosen yarn. This will give you an idea of how your stitch pattern looks in this particular yarn and you can take some time to check for colorfastness and pilling – two items of concern we will address next.

Workshop: How to Test Yarn for Colorfastness

To test yarn for colorfastness, wind a good amount of yarn in a loose hank (or you can use your swatch) and soak in warm/hot water with a small piece of white fabric or a small amount of white yarn. If the dye is likely to bleed, you will see some of the color in the water. Even if you can't see any color in the water, take the items out and squeeze them together, then let dry. If your white fabric or yarn is still white, you're good to go!

Another thing to find out before using a yarn for a handbag is whether or not the yarn will pill. I'm sure you've seen sweaters that took hours, only to pill with one or two wears. Pilling is caused by friction, which is why you will find it often in areas like the underarm of a sweater. The fibers break away from the yarn and then clump into little balls. Since a bag is usually carried under the arm, it is going to get some friction.

How can you tell which yarns will pill? There are a few indicators. First, check the number of plies. The more plies a yarn has, the less likely it is to pill. The fiber content is also indicative of how much a yarn will pill. Cotton, silk and linen aren't likely to pill, but wool and most acrylics are, especially the cheaper acrylics. I would stay away from most acrylics for these types of projects unless you buy an anti-pilling acrylic.

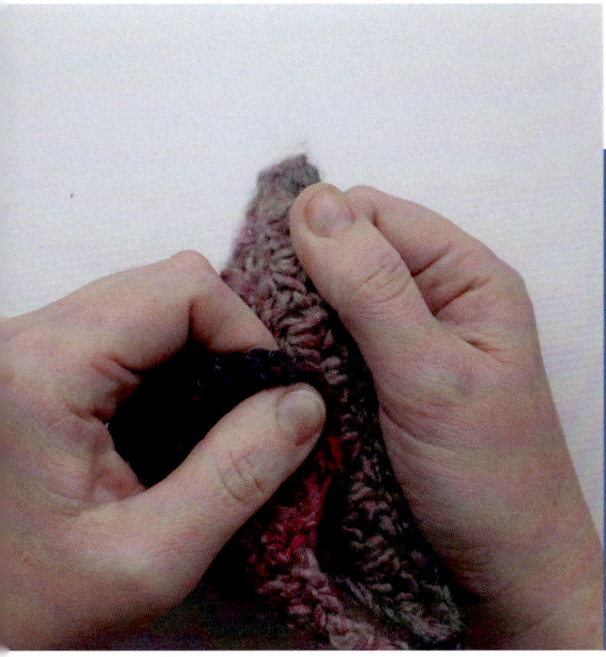

Workshop: How to Test Yarn for Pilling

There are two ways to test yarn for pilling. The first way is to make a swatch and wash it, then rub the fabric together and see if pills begin to form. If the yarn is prone to pilling, it shouldn't take long to see the fibers clumping together.

The second way to test for pilling is to take a few strands of yarn and rub them between your fingers or palms. Get a good amount of friction going on the yarns, then see if the yarn begins to separate or peel apart. You may even see some pilling beginning, especially if the yarns are very prone to pilling. These are indicators that the yarn is not a good fit for a bag that will be carried close to the body.

CHAPTER 3 Basic Finishing *Techniques*

WEAVING IN ENDS

As much as knitters and crocheters hate it, weaving in ends is an essential part of the process. The reason for weaving in ends is to hide the tails of your yarn and make sure they don't come back out again.

Be sure to leave a long tail at the beginning and end of your work, as a small tail is very hard to weave in. I do not recommend working over the yarn tails, as I have found from experience that these ends tend to peek out.

I try as hard as possible to leave the ends at the edges of my work and weave them into the seams. This reduces bulk in the fabric and completely hides the yarn, as the seams are excellent for working the tails into. If possible, I will use my long tail to help seam up the bag and tie it off with the new piece of yarn, hiding it inside the finished bag (between the crocheted fabric and lining fabric, where it will not be seen).

Workshop: Weaving in Ends

If this is not possible, I weave in my ends in the following way:

Step One: Thread the tail through the eye of a tapestry needle.

Step Two: Weave the needle under the bases of a few stitches.

Step Three: Turn, and go back under the same stitches. For extra security, repeat a third time.

Step Four: Clip the yarn close.

BLOCKING

Great finishing begins with blocking. Blocking works best on natural fibers, but even a synthetic fabric can benefit from proper blocking. Some fabrics have to be blocked to achieve the desired result. To open out the stitches and achieve the full size, wet blocking was applied.

When blocking, you use either water or steam to shape your finished piece and allow the fibers to relax. A lot of yarns have chemicals used in processing, and adding moisture to the fibers allows them to open up. Wet blocking makes a crocheted fabric more pliable and able to be shaped to the correct dimensions (given proper gauge).

TOOLS FOR BLOCKING

You will need a few tools for proper blocking, but you don't have to buy anything fancy. You will need pins, such as the T-pins we discussed earlier, although any rust-proof pin will work, a spray bottle, an iron or steamer (for some fabrics), and some crocheters swear by blocking wires, although I have never used them myself.

For a blocking surface, you can pick up a blocking mat or board, or you can use a surface you already have, such as an ironing board, bed, or even just a rug or sofa covered by a sheet.

BLOCKING METHODS

There are several methods you can use to block, and the one you choose will depend upon the fiber content and personal preference.

Wet Blocking

This is by far what I use the most. You can either soak the fabric in a sink or bowl full of water or spray the fabric after it is pinned. With soaking, you will pin the fabric after it is wet, whereas with a spray bottle, you will pin the fabric to shape and then introduce moisture into the fibers. I tend to use the spray method a lot more often, as I like to pin my pieces before they are wet.

There are two methods you can use for wet blocking:

Soaking: Submerge your fabric in a sink or bowl of water, squeeze gently to remove excess water and to allow the water to absorb into the fibers, then place the piece in a towel, roll it up and squeeze to remove excess water. Then, pin to measurements and allow to dry.

Spraying: Use a spray bottle with plain water to deliver the water to your crocheted fabric. Pin the piece to measurements on your blocking surface, then spritz with water until it is as wet as you desire. You want the fibers to become pliable but you don't need them to be soaking wet. If you need, press a towel to the fabric to absorb excess moisture and allow to dry.

Steaming

Steaming uses warmth and moisture to shape crocheted fabrics, and is not appropriate for all fibers. Many natural fibers do well with the warmth as it opens up the fibers. Acrylic also does well with steam, but be careful about touching the surface of the fibers, as a hot iron can scorch or melt fibers if the heating plate is touched to the fabric! Also, if you are using an iron to steam your fabrics, do not lay the fabric down and iron it on an ironing board. This will flatten out your stitches and ruin the fabric.

Steaming dries faster as you are not soaking your fabric, so it can be a good choice if you don't want to wait hours to work with your finished fabric. If you are in doubt about using steam on your project, first check the ball band, then test your swatch. You don't want to apply an improper blocking technique and ruin all your hard work!

Seaming

Seaming is another of those processes that many crafters avoid. I actually like to seam! I find it an enjoyable process to watch my finished pieces come together and create a professional, well-defined piece. With bags, seaming is almost mandatory. There are a few styles of bags you can make where you can get away without seaming, but most of them require at least a couple of seams.

There are several different methods you can use to seam handbags. Luckily, most handbag seams are straight seams, so you don't have to worry about seaming two differently shaped pieces. No matter which method you use to seam, start by lining up your pieces and using safety pins or locking stitch markers to hold the pieces together, making sure the pieces line up nicely. The following seams are my favorites and the ones I use most often.

Workshop: Mattress Stitch

This is the most secure of the hand-sewn stitches, and my favorite method of seaming. This seam is completely invisible from the right side and leaves only a tiny seam on the back side, so there isn't much bulk to this seam.

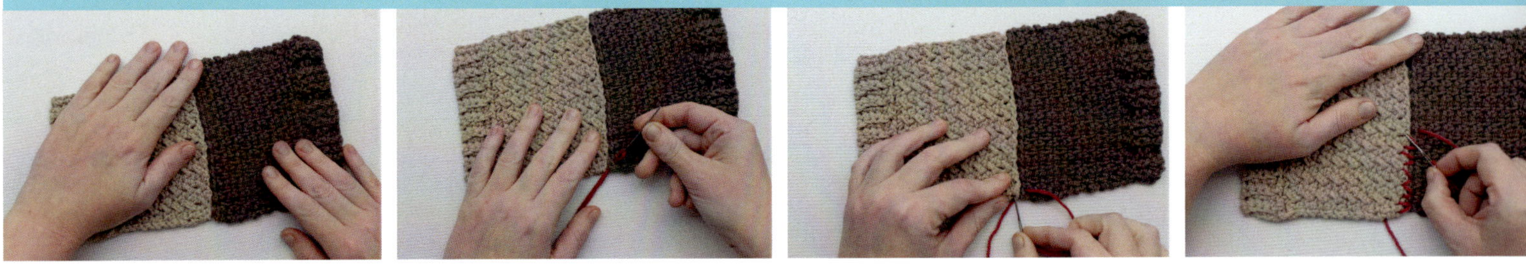

Step One: Lay the pieces with the RS facing you and the edges lined up and even.

Step Two: Thread your yarn needle with the working yarn (contrasting color used here for emphasis).

Step Three: Bring needle up through fabric in the bottom corner, pull yarn through, leaving enough of a tail to weave in later.

Step Four: Insert needle through bottom corner of second piece and pull through.

Step Five: Insert needle back into first side, under the bar of the next stitch or row, pull through.

Step Six: In second piece, insert needle under and through bar of next stitch or row, pull through. Repeat Steps 5 and 6 for length of seam.

Pull tightly as you go to bring the two sides together. You should not be able to see the working yarn.

Workshop: Slip Stitch Seam

This is the other method of seaming that I recommend. If you prefer to do as much as possible with your hook, this is the method for you. It creates less bulk than a single crochet seam and is a good seam for bags, as the added layer of stitching doesn't detract from the design of a handbag, which are often sturdier anyways.

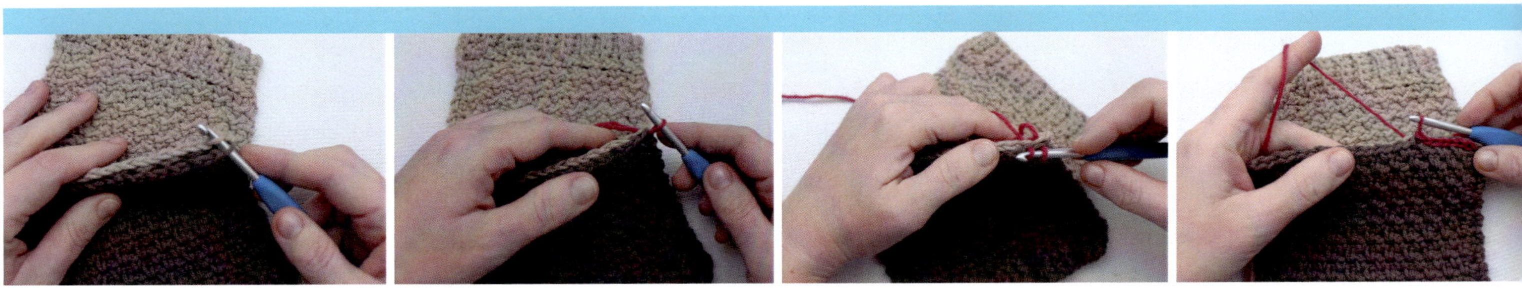

Step One: Hold the fabric with the RS together (WS facing out).

Step Two: Insert hook into a stitch from each side, making sure to only work through one loop from each side.

Step Three: Yarn over and draw through both fabrics **and** the loop on hook.

Step Four: Repeat Steps 2 and 3 for the length of the seam.

CHAPTER 4 Interfacing *and* Linings

To give our bag structure and better functionality, we are going to need to use a lining and some type of stabilizer. Interfacing is the supportive material that hides between the crocheted fabric and the lining fabric. So many times, this critical element is overlooked! To create a truly functional bag, it needs at least a lining, and usually some type of interfacing. How stiff of a structure you want will determine what type of stabilizer or interfacing you want. Let's look at the different types of interfacing before we delve into lining fabrics.

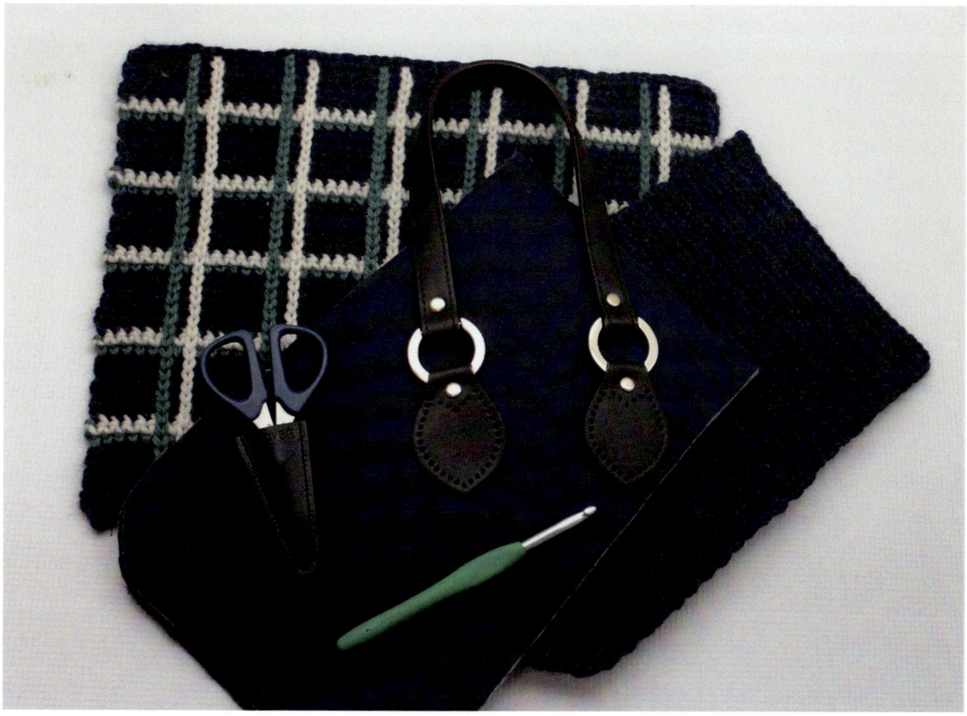

INTERFACING AND STABILIZERS

If you go to your local craft store, you will find many types and weights of interfacing and stabilizer. Fusible, non-fusible, midweight, featherweight and more! It can get very confusing. It took me a long time to find what worked best for me, and you may find that you have to try a few before you get the stability you are looking for.

One thing to note is that you always want a sew-in stabilizer. Fusible stabilizers are meant to be ironed to the fabric, and ironing something you've crocheted is usually not a good idea, no matter what yarn you have used. It flattens the stitches and the yarn itself could be scorched or melted. It's not worth the risk. Fusible interfacing has tiny bumps of glue on it that melt when heat is applied, and since we are not applying heat those bumps are useless. It's best to get a sew-in interfacing that is smooth and just use thread to attach it to the crocheted piece.

Personally, I like the Pellon® 70 Peltex Ultra-Firm Sew-In Stabilizer when I am making a bag that needs a strong shape. Most all the bags you see in this book use this particular type of stabilizer. I have tried crinoline, featherweight and midweight stabilizers and they will work if you aren't looking for a bag that stands up by itself, but if you want serious shaping, go with this type of stabilizer.

There are instances when you would not want to use stabilizer in your bag. If you want a soft shape, such as the *Puff Stitch Clutch* on page 40, you would not need any type of interfacing or stabilizer.

So let's take a look at how to attach stabilizer to your crocheted pieces. This is the same technique you will use for any weight stabilizer.

Workshop How to Attach Stabilizer

Step One: Use crocheted pieces to cut stabilizer slightly smaller than the finished pieces. If there is going to be a fold, cut the lining into a separate piece, as seen in this project.

Step Two: Use a running stitch or backstitch to attach stabilizer to back of crocheted pieces.

LINING FABRICS

Unless you are making a bag with an openwork pattern, I believe a lining is an absolute necessity. Before I used to line my bags, they would stretch out and lose their shape. Even if you choose not to do stabilizer, a lining is essential to making a handbag that looks professional. Don't worry, it's not as hard as it seems.

It's best to choose a lining that compliments your yarn. That doesn't mean the lining has to match it. You can be creative as you want. There are some amazing fabrics out there. I used to always use fabrics made from quilting that were made from cotton, but as I've made more bags, I have found that I like thicker fabrics and often find them in the home decor section of the fabric store.

One of my favorite things that I found while writing this book was quilted fabric in solid colors. The best thing about the quilted fabrics is that they are double sided, so if you have crocheted pieces where the lining shows through, you will still see a nice, finished fabric instead of the back of a fabric. Those are not the only fabrics I use for linings, however. I have also found some heavier weight cottons made for home decor that I love. You can use almost any fabric you like. It's really a matter of personal preference. I've found that the thicker fabrics like the quilted and home decor fabrics make the bag a lot more durable, but you can easily still use lightweight cotton or other fabric. Whatever lining fabric you choose, just be sure it will hold its shape so that there is no stress on the crocheted pieces.

This is where you can really let your personality shine through. A plain black bag a bit boring for you? Try a wild print inside for the lining. Love florals? How about a beautiful floral lining inside your bag? There really is no right or wrong, so feel free to get creative.

Workshop — How to Create a Lining

Use the finished crochet pieces to find measurements. Draw slightly outside crocheted pieces. If possible, create as few lining pieces as you can, such as with this coin purse. The lining was created after the bottom seam was sewn. Cut pieces to measurements.

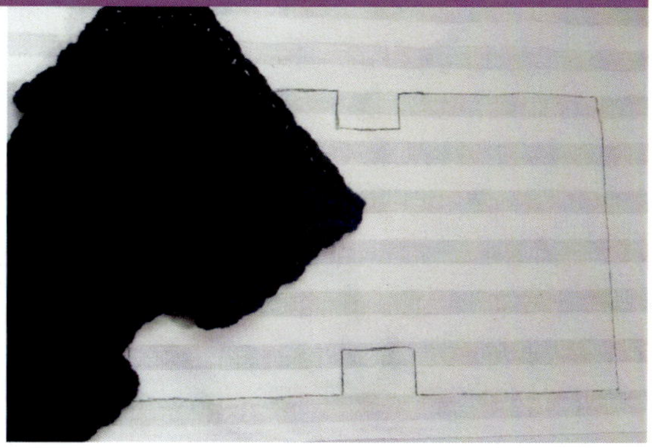

Tips & Tricks

When working around a curve, you will need to clip your fabric. This is a technique commonly used in sewing and allows the curve to lie flat. There are different techniques for inward vs. outward curves. For inward curves, clip the curve every ½-¾" (12-19 mm) - along the curve after you have seamed – but be very careful not to clip into your seam! For outward curves, create V-shaped notches in the seam allowance every ½" (12 mm). This will reduce bulk and allow the seam to lie flat.

Workshop — How to Attach a Lining

Step One: Bring the yarn from the inside of the lining, where the knot will be hidden between the lining fabric and the outer shell. Take a small stitch from the crocheted fabric. I try to go through one crocheted stitch.

Step Two: Take a small stitch from the lining fabric.

Work back and forth taking a small stitch from the body of the bag followed by a small stitch from the lining fabric. When pulled tight (but not too tightly or it will pucker), this creates a nearly invisible join.

CHAPTER 5 Handles *and* Hardware

Nothing can bring your handbag up to designer quality faster than good handles and hardware. Luckily, there are many options today for handmade handbags, from leather and fabric to many different hardware finishes (including rose gold!) and everything in between. Sometimes the choice can seem overwhelming. Take some time examining handles and hardware before you begin your project. Little details make a big difference.

HANDLES

You have two main options when choosing a handle for your bag – purchased or crocheted. You can choose to buy or create your handles, and there are times when either will look fantastic. The choice is really up to you and it all comes down to personal preference.

PURCHASED HANDLES

These are pre-made handles usually out of leather, fabric, wood or another material. You will see leather handles used in many projects throughout this book, many of which already contained the metal hardware on the handles, making them easy to attach with minimal effort. I find that these types of handles always give a project a more professional look, and I also find them easier than crocheted handles because you don't have to make the handles at all – just attach and you are ready to go!

Most purchased handles that are attached directly to the bag come with pre-drilled holes for easy sewing. The key is to sew the handles on before you attach the lining but after the craft stabilizer. This gives the handle a supportive structure to attach to, but by waiting to put in the lining, you will hide the back of your stitches because the lining fabric will cover them up.

Workshop: How to Attach Purchased Handles

I always buy purchased handles that already have the holes for easy sewing. This allows me to attach the handle to the bag with minimal fuss. Always sew in your craft stabilizer before attaching a handle for greater stability!

Step One: Position the handle in the proper place.

Step Two: Thread sewing needle with double length of thread and bring up from the wrong side of the fabric.

Step Three: Bring needle down through next hole.

Step Four: Bring needle up in next hole. Continue working in and out in all holes of the handle. To finish, bring needle to the back and tie off.

CROCHETED HANDLES

There are two ways I like to make crocheted handles that stand up to wear. I can't stand for my handles to droop or sag, which they will if the bag is too heavy. With a bit of rope or nylon webbing, we can create handles that are crocheted to match our bag but also stand up to daily wear and tear.

If I want a flat handle, I will buy nylon webbing/strap at my local craft store. You can get this in several different widths and colors to suit your needs. I tend to try and find a color as close to the bag as possible and usually leave the nylon showing on the back of the strap. You can also try covering the nylon with crochet on the front and back, but from my experience, anything worsted weight or heavier will just make too bulky a strap if you do it this way.

Working a crocheted strap this way is easy. It is worked flat and then stitched to the nylon. Most straps aren't that wide, so it works up quite fast. This is an excellent way to ensure that your strap matches your yarn.

Workshop: How to Make a Strap with Nylon Webbing

Nylon webbing or strapping is a wonderful way to add structure and support to flat handles. It comes in several widths and can be simply sewn to the back or it can be tucked away neatly inside a double layer of crochet, such as the straps for the *Tapestry Drawstring Backpack* on page 50.

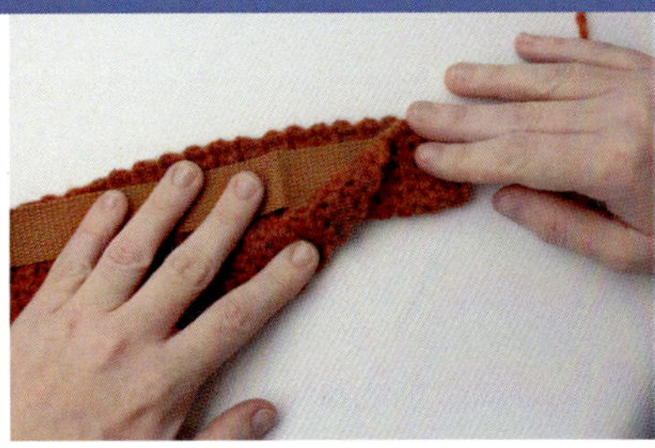

Step One: To create a strap with a double thickness, crochet a piece twice as wide as the nylon webbing.

Step Two: Fold webbing in half and place the nylon inside.

Step Three: Stitch through the end of the nylon to hold in place.

Step Four: Use the mattress stitch to close up the side seam.

The other way I make straps is to get a piece of strong rope or cord, such as jute, and make a crocheted tube around the rope. This way is also easy and ensures that the strap matches the finished bag exactly. You crochet a flat piece of fabric, place the rope or cord inside, and seam up the strap. This gives you a rounded "rolled" strap.

Workshop: How to Make a Strap with Cord

These cords come in many different widths so you can customize the size of your strap. I used a larg cord for the *Tote with Zipper Pocket* on page 42.

Step One: Crochet a piece wide enough to wrap around the cord and the same length as the cord.

Step Two: Place the cord inside the crocheted strap.

Step Three: Use the mattress stitch (see page 18) to sew seam closed.

HARDWARE

Great hardware can really make a bag stand out. This is what separates the ordinary, hobby maker's handbag to a really professional-looking bag. Little details do go a long way. Things such as purse feet, clasps, buckles, and grommets can take your bag from ordinary to extraordinary. Let's take a look at each of these things in detail.

PURSE FEET

Bags get a lot of wear and tear on the bottom from being set down on all types of surfaces. This can affect your bag bottom, especially if it's made from yarn and not a purchased base. Purse feet can help minimize the wear on a bag base because the feet take the brunt of the friction, saving the yarn from some of the wear. You can't completely keep a bag from wear and tear as you use it, but things like these can certainly minimize it. If you put hours into a handbag, you want it to look good as long as possible. Luckily, purse feet are inexpensive and easy to insert.

GROMMETS

Grommets are metal rings that reinforce a hole made in the fabric. They can be purely decorative or they can be functional. Instead of just having a hole in your crocheted piece, grommets give a finished look and intentionality to a small opening. One way I like to use grommets is to weave a piece of ribbon through them. You can find grommets that need to be hammered in place, which work well, or you can find the ones with screws, such as I used in the *Grommet Bag* on page 46.

Workshop: How to Attach a Grommet

For this workshop, I'm using the type of grommet that has 2 small screws. I found these much easier to work with than grommets that required a special tool or that you have to hammer together.

Step One: Position grommet in chain space.

Step Two: Ensure that the two screw holes are clear.

Step Three: Use a small screwdriver to screw in the tiny screws that come with the grommets.

BUCKLES

Buckles can act as a closure or they can be decorative. I like to use them for both functions, depending upon the bag. Luckily, these are as easy to apply as purchased handles. Most leather or pleather buckles have pre-drilled holes just like the handles. Many places sell handles and buckles that match, which is great for giving a professional look to your bags.

The key to buckles is making sure you line them up properly. Check and double check that the buckle will match up the way you want it to when the bag is finished. Buckles are another thing you will need to attach before the bag is completely put together, so placement can be a bit tricky. Buckles should be sewn in at the same time as handles – after you put the craft stabilizer in, but before you sew the seams or attach the lining.

You attach a buckle the same way you do purchased handles, working through the pre-made holes with a double strand of yarn.

PURSE FRAMES

A purse frame is another great way to take an ordinary crochet project and turn it into something special. I love to use these for clutches. Most frames double as closures, so you are getting more bang for your buck when you use a frame. It gives stability and structure to your bag while also serving as the way to keep the bag closed.

There are several types of purse frames and my favorite are the sew-in frames. There are ones that can be glued as well, but I'm hesitant to try and glue anything to my crocheted pieces. It's not that easy to start over if you make a mistake! So, for this reason, I stick to the sew-in frames. I like the look of the matching thread when I sew in a frame better anyways.

Frames also come in lots of different sizes and shapes, so the sky is the limit when choosing a frame for your handcrafted handbag. Curved, straight, plain, fancy – you name it, you can probably find it.

Workshop: How to Attach a Sew-In Purse Frame

Step One: Line up fabric with frame.

Step Two: Position crocheted fabric and lining fabric inside frame where the edges will be hidden.

Step Three: Bring thread up from back through first hole in frame, being sure to catch both fabrics.

Step Four: Use a back stitch to secure all holes of frame through both layers of fabric. Tie off.

BAG BASES

You can buy pre-made bases that already have holes to work into, and these make for wonderfully sturdy foundations for bags. Each of these bases will have a different number of holes to crochet into, so take this into account when making a pattern that uses a bag bottom/ base.

Workshop: How to Use a Bag Base

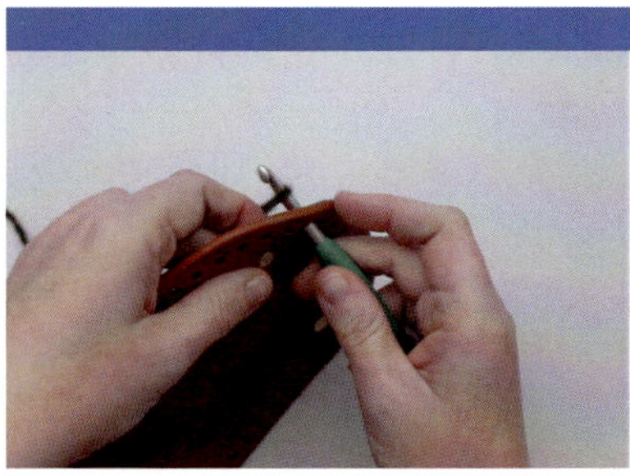
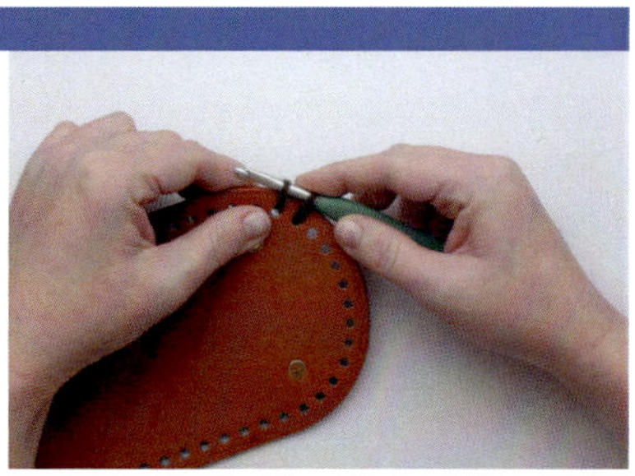

Step One: Hold base with **right** side facing you. Insert hook and pull a loop through. If your working hook is too large, use a smaller hook for this step, then change to larger hook for the stitch.

Step Two: Work the stitch of your choice, always moving to the next hole in the bag base.

CHAPTER 6 Closures

Most bags benefit greatly from some type of closure. Closures serve to keep your belongings safely inside, and also add to the beauty and structure of the bag. When I design a bag, I always think about the style of bag it is and what closures would work the best. Some bags, of course, don't have closures at all, such as totes and market bags, but others would be naked without them.

My favorite closures for bags are zippers, buttons, toggles and snaps. Many times a closure has inspired an entire bag design. I love finding unique items to use on my projects. A special button or toggle closure can really make a design. Spend some time finding just the right closure for your bag. You won't regret it.

ZIPPERS

When I was in college, I majored in fashion design. One of the things I hated most was sewing in zippers – and I often asked my mom to hand sew them in for me! I always tried to cut corners in those days, and wanted only to use my machine. Now that I'm more experienced, I love hand sewing. In fact, no machine was used to make any of these projects! I even sewed my linings by hand. I have learned to love hand sewing, especially putting in zippers.

One of the major mistakes I kept making when first designing bags was getting the fabric too close to the zipper teeth. There needs to be a decent amount of space between the yarn or fabric and the zipper teeth. This not only serves to allow the zipper to open and close without catching, it also just plain looks better. In the workshop, I'll show you the proper way to sew in a zipper.

There are many different types of zippers available, and with bags, it is really a personal preference. A lot of times I use sturdy zippers with metal teeth, which matches the other hardware on my bag. If you have any type of metallic elements on your bag, you should ensure they match as closely as possible. For my Cabled Handbag I chose a zipper with antique brass and made sure that any metal elements, even the purse feet, matched the finish.

Other zippers that I like to use are the zippers by the yard from Sallie Tomato. These look metallic, but aren't, making them easy to cut to length. The matching zipper pulls that come with these zippers by the yard make it easy to create a zipper in any length or style you need. These were my preference when needing a zipper that met in the center.

I don't often buy zippers that fit my measurements exactly, because with a handbag you close up the ends anyway. When I am getting a zipper for a garment, I make sure it is the exact measurement I need, because I want the end to have a finished look. With a bag, if the zipper is too long, I simply cut it off and add a thread stop to the end, which is covered by the bag itself.

You can get zippers in almost any color you can imagine. They do not have to match the bag. I like mine in neutral colors that compliment my yarn, but you can put in any zipper color you like. Hot pink, lime green, or turquoise are all options when you make your own bag.

Workshop How to Apply a Zipper

Zippers should be applied after the craft stabilizer but before any seaming or lining has been done. I sew my zippers to the main fabric and the lining separately to ensure even, almost invisible stitches.

Gather all of your materials before you begin. Pins, sewing needle, thread that matches your yarn, the pieces you will be sewing the zipper to, and, of course, the zipper itself. Be sure that whatever thread you are using will hide in your yarn. You don't want to run the risk of sewing the zipper in place, only to find that you can see every stitch through the yarn.

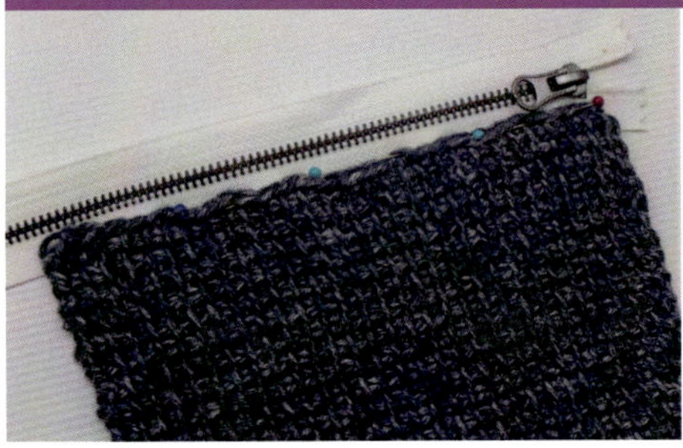

Step One: Pin the zipper in place.

After your finished pieces are secured to the craft stabilizer, lay them out flat with the zipper edges together. With the zipper closed, use pins to secure the zipper in place. Before you begin stitching, double check that the zipper is exactly where it needs to be. Unzip it, measure it and be absolutely sure the zipper is where it needs to be. The zipper stop at the top should be even with the edge of your crocheted fabric.

Step Two: Stitch the first side.

Thread your needle and tie a knot at the end. Bring your thread up from the bottom of the zipper. This end will be covered by the lining fabric, so no need to worry about hiding this little knot. Make a small stitch in your crocheted fabric, then a tiny stitch in the zipper tape. Work back and forth, taking a small stitch from the crochet, then a small stitch from the zipper tape. For best results, use very, very small stitches. I often catch just a couple of threads of the zipper tape so that I can get as many stitches in as possible, making the zipper secure but also hiding the stitches as much as possible. Continue this way all the way to the end, then tie a knot securely at the end, hiding this knot as well.

Step Three: Sew the second side.

Repeat the same procedure from step two to attach the second side, making sure to also begin at the same end of the zipper. If you started from the bottom of the zipper for the first side, be sure to sew from the bottom on the second side.

Step Four: Repeat for the lining.

To attach the lining fabric, fold the top edge down (you may iron this if desired but it is not necessary), then thread your needle and tie a knot. Bring the thread up from the inside of the lining to hide the knot, and begin sewing the same way you sewed in the crocheted piece. Take a tiny stitch out of the lining, then the zipper, all the way to the end, keeping the fabric the same distance away from the zipper teeth as the yarn. Work one side at a time same as the steps above.

After following these steps, you would be ready to move on to other steps in the finishing process. Handles should be sewn on after a zipper, but if you do it in the opposite order it doesn't affect things that much. After the zipper is in, you could sew on any buckles, purse feet, or other hardware. Then, you are ready to move on to the next step, which would be to sew the lining.

BUTTONS

I love collecting buttons. There are so many sizes, shapes and materials. Often, when I am making a design and need a button, I have just the one in my stash. Sometimes, however, I will design an item just around a particular button design. I love how they can add an extra element to crochet and enjoy picking ones that stand out.

There are many different types of buttons, so let's take a moment to discuss them here. They can be made in almost any material, but my favorite are wood or plastic.

There are two main styles of buttons: flat buttons with holes for sewing and shank buttons. Flat buttons have either two or four holes that you use to sew through, keeping the button securely attached to the fabric. Shank buttons, on the other hand, are only sewn on the back through what is called the shank, and you don't see the sewing yarn or thread on the front.

Also keep in mind the size of the buttons. There are many different sizes, so be sure you are following the pattern and picking out the right size button for the hole that will be made in the pattern. If the buttons are purely decorative, however, this isn't a concern. For a functional button, check your pattern directions carefully.

When choosing buttons for crocheted items, there are a few things to keep in mind. Firstly, make sure the buttons can be attached easily. I tend to look for larger holes in my buttons so I can use some of the working yarn to secure them. Often, if I have a yarn with more than one ply, I will separate the plies and use two (if possible) to sew the buttons on. If the holes are too small, you will have to attach the button with a sewing needle and thread, which is fine depending upon the look you are going for.

Workshop: *How to Sew On a Flat Button*

For truly functional flat buttons, you need to create a thread shank, which can be accomplished by first putting a tapestry needle underneath your button and later wrapping thread underneath the button. This lifts the button off the fabric and allows the button to not pull tightly when the fabric is closed.

Step One: Place button in desired location with tapestry needle underneath. Be sure tapestry needle stays directly underneath the center of the button.

Step Two: Bring the needle with thread or yarn from **back** to **front** and through one hole of the button.

Step Three: Insert needle through second hole and bring needle down from **front** to **back**, working over the tapestry needle.

Repeat Steps 2 and 3 several times. There is no rule on how many times to sew a button. I just keep repeating until it looks right to me, which may be as few as four times for thicker yarn/thread or more for smaller sewing thread.

If you have a button with four holes, you will want to work in an "x" pattern, working the same two diagonal holes several times, and then coming back to the other side several times. Working it this way gives the button a more polished finish than working the thread like an equal sign or working back and forth in the "x" pattern.

Step Four: Remove tapestry needle, bring yarn up underneath the button and wrap around the threads several times, creating a thread shank.

Step Five: Secure the thread by weaving the thread through the back of the fabric the same way you would weave in ends. Tie off and cut with scissors.

Workshop: How to Sew On a Shank Button

Shank buttons are made where they do not lie flat against the fabric. The "shank" of a button is the part behind it that gives it room to move and to allow the second layer of fabric to lie flat. Shank buttons are easy to sew on.

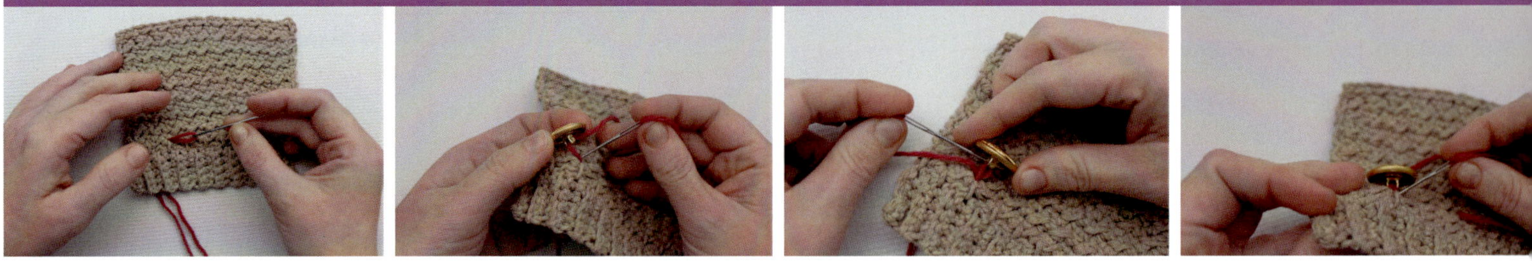

Step One: Bring yarn up from back of fabric in location desired.

Step Two: Pull needle and thread through the shank, then insert needle into same spot on fabric and pull through to back.

Step Three: Continue looping yarn through shank and back through fabric in the same spot until secure. Tie off in back of fabric.

TOGGLES

A toggle, traditionally, is a short rod of wood sewn to one side of a garment, usually a coat, with a loop on the other side. Toggles make great closures on coats, but they also do very well as closures on bags. Attaching a toggle is much like sewing on a button. Toggles usually have one or two holes used to attach securely to the fabric and must be sewn in.

Workshop: How to Attach a Toggle

Step One: Determine placement of toggle.

Step Two: Bring needle up from back of fabric and into first hole of toggle.

Step Three: Bring needle down into second hole to back of fabric.

Step Four: Repeat Steps 2 and 3 several times until toggle is secure. Wrap yarn around underneath toggle a few times to create a shank, similar to sewing on a flat button. Bring yarn or thread to back and tie off.

SNAPS

Regular snaps are not a closure I use often, but magnetic snaps are perfect for closing handbags. They come in a variety of finishes and sizes, so you are sure to find one that can fit your bag design. I used a couple of different styles of magnetic snaps for the projects in this book. A few are sewn in, similar to the buckles and handles with pre-drilled holes. Others need small holes cut in the fabric for prongs to attach on the back of the fabric. Both of them work the same and are easy to attach. Since we have already done a couple of workshops showing how to attach items with pre-drilled holes, we will look at how to attach the other snaps.

Workshop — How to Attach Magnetic Snaps

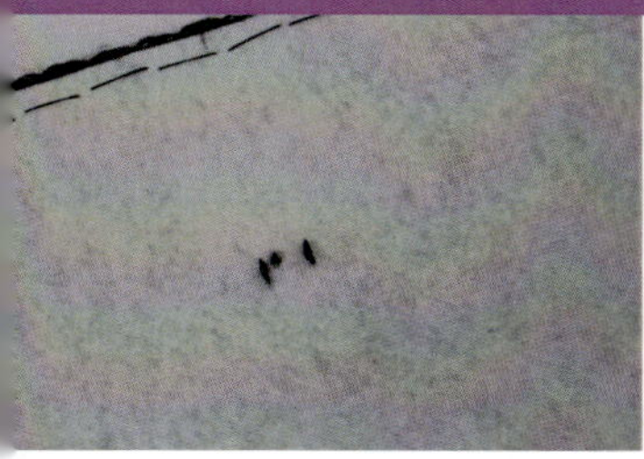

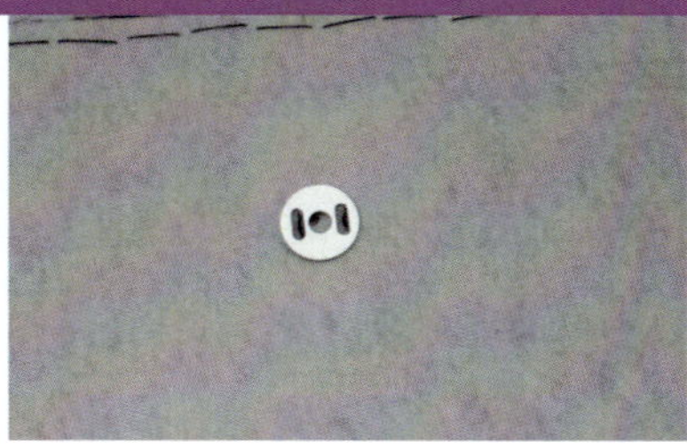

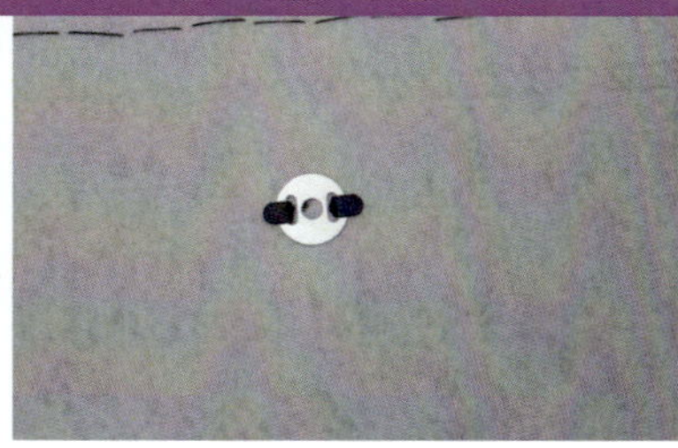

Step One: Mark placement of snap. You can use the back of the snap as a guide if desired.

Step Two: Cut small holes and push prongs through. (It is better to err on the side of too small than too large).

Step Three: Place back on prongs and bend prongs to side.

Convertible Clutch instructions available in #7915

CHAPTER 7 Special *Techniques*

There are a few techniques that don't really fall into any other category, but are ones that can add that extra special touch to a handcrafted handbag. I love taking small details into account when designing, and often will add a small finishing touch to my bags, such as adding pockets, using pom poms or tassels, or even trying out a special technique like tapestry crochet or surface slip stitch.

These are all things that can take your bag from handmade to professional. Use a pom pom or tassel on your zipper pull. Work in some beautiful colors with tapestry crochet or surface slip stitch. The possibilities are endless when making your own bag.

Let's delve into each of these topics separately.

Barrel Bag instructions available in #7918

POCKETS

Who doesn't love pockets in their bags? When you make your own bag, you can add as many pockets as you want! While we can't discuss all the types of pockets that are out there, we can look at several different ones made from the crocheted fabric. Of course, you can always make pockets in your linings, just look up some of the wonderful sewing tutorials available.

Cabled Handbag instructions available in #7918

SIDE POCKETS

These are an easy way to add functionality to your project. You simply create a match to your side panel that is shorter and then treat the two as one.

CENTER POCKETS

These pockets are usually written into the pattern. This type of pocket depends upon a separate piece made to go behind the fabric. Once you create the lining of the pocket, you will work across those stitches when the pattern indicates. I love using this type of pocket in my bags, as it adds to the design characteristics as well as the functionality.

PATCH POCKETS

This is a very simple way to add a pocket to anything. It's simply a pocket made separately and sewn on. You see these on garments all the time, but they are also very usable on bags. These pockets are made separately and then sewn on. You can choose to use craft stabilizer and lining for this pocket if you wish, but it is just as nice without.

Of course, any of these pockets could also be found on the interior of the bag if you wished to skip the lining – the choice is totally up to you!

TAPESTRY CROCHET

This type of crochet is gaining in popularity, and it's easy to see why. Instead of carrying floating strands on the back of your work, you simply work over the strands you are not using. You can create some amazing colorwork patterns using tapestry crochet. This technique is used in the *Tapestry Drawstring Backpack* on page 50.

Workshop | Surface Slip Stitch

SURFACE SLIP STITCH

This technique is used to add a design to the surface of a project. It's a great way to outline a tapestry crochet project or it can be used in creative ways to make letters or other decorative shapes.

Step One: Pull up a loop from the back of the fabric.

Step Two: Insert hook into the next st and pull up another loop.

Step Three: Pull this loop through the first loop on the hook. Continue pulling up a single loop and pulling it through.

POM POMS

While pom poms often have the reputation as being childish or just for beanies, I have found that a properly placed pom can really add a nice touch to a bag. It can add a decorative element if used as a zipper pull or on the corner of a bag. Play around with pom poms and you just might find yourself really enjoying them.

TASSELS

Tassels are all over the place in home decor, and for good reason. They add such a nice decorative touch to crochet projects. I'm sure you're used to seeing them on shawls and pillows, but consider adding them to handbags in the same way as pom poms. Use them as zipper pulls, on the corner of your bags, or adorning a flap.

FINAL THOUGHTS ABOUT HANDBAGS

There is nothing quite like carrying a handbag you have put heart and soul into. A bag where you have lovingly placed each stitch with care. A bag that has the exact handles and hardware you wanted, along with a beautiful yarn that spoke to you. It may be hard work, but the end result is so worth it.

I hope by now you have an idea of how handbags are made and what makes a handcrafted handbag different from just a crocheted one. The stabilizer, lining, attention to detail. All of these things matter. I hope you not only make the designs in this book, but that you branch out into creating a handbag that perfectly matches what you need.

This method of handbags is the one that I use and love, but don't be afraid to branch out and find what materials and techniques work best for you. You may find a different stabilizer or type of lining you like. Don't be afraid to experiment and try new things!

I hope you have learned new techniques and skills that you can carry with you as you move forward in your crochet journey. Remember to always pay attention to details, as these can make or break a project, and always strive for the best construction possible. I used to try and cut corners, but have learned since to take it slow. I always love my finished items so much more this way.

Above all, never quit learning. This amazing hobby is always changing and there is always something new to learn, something new to make. I hope you find inspiration wherever you go.

Intermediate *Patterns*

Diamond *Coin Purse*

This small project uses basic construction techniques, but the difficulty of the stitch pattern brings it up to an intermediate level.

INTERMEDIATE

Finished Size: Approximately 5½" wide x 4" tall x 1" deep (14 cm x 10 cm x 2.5 cm)

WHAT YOU'LL NEED:

Yarn (Fine Weight)

FINE 2

[1.75 ounces, 136 yards (50 grams, 125 meters) per ball**]**:

- ☐ 1 ball

Crochet Hook

- ☐ Size H (5 mm) **or** size needed for gauge

Notions

- ☐ Craft stabilizer
- ☐ Lining fabric (Hobby Lobby)
- ☐ Zipper (Sallie Tomato white and gold)
- ☐ Yarn needle
- ☐ Sewing needle & matching thread

GAUGE INFORMATION

In pattern,
20 sts and 16 rows = 4" (10 cm)

Gauge Swatch: 6" wide x 2" high (15.25 cm x 5 cm)

Work same as Side Panel, page 34, for 8 rows: 30 sts.

STITCH GUIDE

FRONT POST TREBLE CROCHET *(abbreviated FPtr)*

YO twice, insert hook from **front** to **back** around post of st indicated ***(Fig. 6, page 62)***, YO and pull up a loop (4 loops on hook), (YO and draw through 2 loops on hook) 3 times. Skip dc **behind** FPtr.

FRONT POST TREBLE CROCHET 2 TOGETHER *(abbreviated FPtr2tog)*

First Leg: YO twice, insert hook from **front** to **back** around post of st indicated 2 rows **below *(Fig. 6, page 62)***, YO and pull up a loop (4 loops on hook), (YO and draw through 2 loops on hook) twice (2 loops on hook).

Second Leg: YO twice, skip next 3 sts 2 rows **below**, insert hook from **front** to **back** around post of next st 2 rows **below**, YO and pull up a loop (5 loops on hook), (YO and draw through 2 loops on hook) twice, YO and draw through all 3 loops on hook. Skip dc **behind** FPtr2tog.

SIDE PANEL (Make 2)

Beginning at top edge, ch 31.

Row 1 (RS)**:** Working in back ridge of chs ***(Fig. 2, page 62)***, sc in second ch from hook and in each ch across: 30 sc.

Note: Loop a short piece of yarn around any stitch to mark Row 1 as **right** side.

Row 2: Ch 3 **(counts as first dc, now and throughout)**, turn; dc in next sc and in each sc across.

Row 3: Ch 1, turn; work FPtr around third sc on Row 1, sc in next 3 dc, beginning around same sc on Row 1 as previous FPtr, work FPtr2tog, ★ sc in next 3 dc, beginning around same sc on Row 1 as Second Leg of previous post st, work FPtr2tog; repeat from ★ across to last 5 sts, sc in next 3 sts, FPtr around same sc as Second Leg of previous post st, sc in last dc.

Row 4: Ch 3, turn; dc in next st and in each st across.

Row 5: Ch 1, turn; sc in first 2 dc, beginning around first post st 2 rows **below**, work FPtr2tog, sc in next 3 dc, ★ working around same st as Second Leg of previous post st, work FPtr2tog, sc in next 3 dc; repeat from ★ across.

Row 6: Ch 3, turn; dc in next st and in each st across.

Row 7: Ch 1, turn; FPtr around first post st 2 rows **below**, ★ sc in next 3 dc, working around same st as Second Leg of previous post st, work FPtr2tog; repeat from ★ to last 5 sts, sc in next 3 dc, FPtr around same st as Second Leg of previous post st, sc in last dc.

Rows 8-15: Repeat Rows 4-7 twice.

Row 16: Turn; slip st in first 4 sts, ch 1, sc in next st and in each st across to last 4 sts, leave last 4 sts unworked: 22 sc.

Rows 17-20: Ch 1, turn; sc in each sc across.

Finish off.

FINISHING

Use finished pieces to cut craft stabilizer and lining fabric.
Sew craft stabilizer to **wrong** side of Side Panels.
Sew zipper in place.
Using working yarn sew side, bottom edge and side seams.
Sew lining fabric in place.

Double Zipper Travel Bag

The addition of a second zipper brings this simple bag up to an intermediate level. To make this bag with two sections, simply add a divider to the lining fabric.

INTERMEDIATE

Finished Size: Approximately 11" wide x 6½" tall x 4" deep (28 cm x 16.5 cm x 10 cm)

WHAT YOU'LL NEED:

Yarn (Light Weight)

LIGHT 3

[1.75 ounces, 95 yards (50 grams, 87 meters) per ball**]**:

- ☐ MC (Grey) - 1 ball
- ☐ CC1 (Black) - 1 ball
- ☐ CC2 (Blue/Grey) - 1 ball
- ☐ CC3 (Blue) - 1 ball

Crochet Hook

- ☐ Size H (5 mm) **or** size needed for gauge

Notions

- ☐ Craft stabilizer
- ☐ Lining fabric
- ☐ Zipper - 2
- ☐ Yarn needle
- ☐ Sewing needle & matching thread

GAUGE INFORMATION

In pattern (modified bean st), 18 sts and 16 rows = 4" (10 cm)

Gauge Swatch: 4¼" wide x 4" high (10.75 cm x 10 cm)

With MC, ch 21.

Work same as Main Panel, page 38, without changing colors: 10 mbs and 9 chs (19 sts **total**).

Finish off.

STITCH GUIDE

MODIFIED BEAN STITCH

(abbreviated mbs) (uses one st)

Insert hook in st indicated, YO and pull up a loop, YO, insert hook in **same** st, YO and pull up a loop (4 loops on hook), YO and draw through all 4 loops on hook.

MODIFIED BEAN STITCH 2 TOGETHER

(abbreviated mbs2tog) (uses 3 sts)

Insert hook in mbs indicated, YO and pull up loop, YO, skip **next** ch, insert hook in **next** mbs, YO and pull up loop (4 loops on hook), YO and draw through all 4 loops on hook.

MAIN PANEL (Make 2)

With MC and beginning at bottom edge, ch 51.

Row 1 (RS)**:** Work mbs in third ch from hook, ★ ch 1, skip next ch, work mbs in next ch; repeat from ★ across changing to CC3 in last mbs ***(Fig. 5b, page 63)***: 25 mbs and 24 chs (49 sts **total**).

Note: Loop a short piece of yarn around any stitch to mark Row 1 as **right** side.

Begin working in Stripe Sequence as follows: (4 Rows CC3, 2 rows MC) twice, 4 rows CC2, 2 rows MC, 4 rows CC2, 3 rows MC.

Rows 2-23: Ch 2 (does **not** count as a st), turn; work mbs in first mbs, ★ ch 1, skip next ch, work mbs in next mbs; repeat from ★ across.

Rows 24-26: Ch 2 (does **not** count as a st), turn; beginning in first mbs, work mbs2tog, ch 1, ★ skip next ch, work mbs in next mbs, ch 1; repeat from ★ across to last 4 sts, skip next ch, beginning in next mbs, work mbs2tog: 37 sts.

Finish off.

SIDE PANEL (Make 2)

With MC and beginning at bottom edge, ch 19.

Row 1 (RS)**:** Work mbs in third ch from hook, ★ ch 1, skip next ch, work mbs in next ch; repeat from ★ across changing to CC3 in last mbs: 9 mbs and 8 chs (17 sts **total**).

Note: Mark Row 1 as **right** side.

Begin working in Stripe Sequence as follows: (4 Rows CC3, 2 rows MC) twice, 4 rows CC2, 2 rows MC.

Rows 2-13: Ch 2 (does **not** count as a st), turn; work mbs in first mbs, ★ ch 1, skip next ch, work mbs in next mbs; repeat from ★ across.

Finish off.

CENTER PANEL

With CC2, ch 71.

Row 1 (RS)**:** Working in back ridge of chs ***(Fig. 2, page 62)***, work mbs in third ch from hook, ★ ch 1, skip next ch, work mbs in next ch; repeat from ★ across: 35 mbs and 34 chs (69 sts **total**).

Note: Mark Row 1 as **right** side.

Rows 2-7: Ch 2 (does **not** count as a st), turn; work mbs in first mbs, ★ ch 1, skip next ch, work mbs in next mbs; repeat from ★ across.

Finish off.

BOTTOM PANEL

With CC1, ch 51.

Row 1 (RS)**:** Work mbs in third ch from hook, ★ ch 1, skip next ch, work mbs in next ch; repeat from ★ across: 25 mbs and 24 chs (49 sts **total**).

Note: Mark Row 1 as **right** side.

Rows 2-17: Ch 2 (does **not** count as a st), turn; work mbs in first mbs, ★ ch 1, skip next ch, work mbs in next mbs; repeat from ★ across.

Finish off.

FINISHING

Use finished pieces to cut craft stabilizer and lining fabric.
Sew craft stabilizer to **wrong** side of Main Panels, Side Panels, Center Panel and Bottom Panel.
Use working yarn to sew Bottom and Side Panels together.
Sew zipper along each side of Center Panel.
Sew zipper from Row 15 on one side of Main Panel, across top of Main Panel, down thru Row 15 on second side to Row 15.
Repeat with second Main Panel.
Use working yarn to sew end of Center Panel to side Panels.
Sew lining pieces together same as bag.
Sew lining fabric in place.
Use working yarn to sew Main Panels to Bottom Panel.

Puff Stitch *Clutch*

This little clutch relies on a quilted fabric and a purse frame for its structure.

INTERMEDIATE

Finished Size: Approximately 8" wide x 5" high x 1½" deep (20.5 cm x 12.5 cm x 4 cm)

WHAT YOU'LL NEED:

Yarn (Medium Weight) MEDIUM 4

[3.5 ounces, 151 yards (100 grams, 138 meters) per hank]:

- ☐ 1 hank

Crochet Hook

- ☐ Size I (5.5 mm) **or** size needed for gauge

Notions

- ☐ Quilted lining fabric
- ☐ 8" (20.5 cm) Purse frame
- ☐ Yarn needle
- ☐ Sewing needle & matching thread

GAUGE INFORMATION

In pattern (Puff St),
13 sts and 9 rows = 4" (10 cm)
Gauge Swatch: 4¼" wide x 2¼" high (10.75 cm x 5.75 cm)
Ch 16.
Work same as Main Panel for 5 rows: 7 Puff Sts and 7 sps.
Finish off.

STITCH GUIDE

PUFF ST (uses one st or sp)
YO, insert in st or sp indicated, YO and pull up a loop (3 loops on hook), ★ YO, insert in **same** st or sp, YO and pull up a loop; repeat from ★ 2 times **more** (9 loops on hook), YO and draw through all 9 loops on hook.

MAIN PANEL (Make 2)

Ch 32.

Row 1 (RS)**:** Work Puff St in fourth ch from hook, ★ ch 1, skip next ch, work Puff St in next ch; repeat from ★ across: 15 Puff Sts and 15 sps.

Note: Loop a short piece of yarn around any stitch to mark Row 1 as **right** side.

Rows 2-7: Ch 3, turn; ★ work Puff St in next ch-1 sp, ch 1, skip next Puff St; repeat from ★ across, work Puff St in last ch-3 sp.

Row 8: Turn; slip st in next ch-1 sp and in next Puff St, ch 3, work Puff St in next ch-1 sp, ★ ch 1, skip next Puff St, work Puff St in next ch-1 sp; repeat from ★ across to last ch-1 sp, leave last ch-1 sp unworked: 13 Puff Sts and 13 sps.

Rows 9-11: Ch 3, turn; ★ work Puff St in next ch-1 sp, ch 1, skip next Puff St; repeat from ★ across, work Puff St in last ch-3 sp.

Finish off.

FINISHING

Use finished pieces to cut lining fabric.
Sew sides and bottom of lining and bag.
Sew purse frame to top, making sure to work through lining and crocheted fabric.

Tote with Zipper Pocket

The addition of a zippered pocket to one of the panels makes this bag more functional. The Colorscape yarn with the mixed cluster stitch pattern gives this bag visual interest.

INTERMEDIATE

Finished Size: Approximately 12" wide x 9" tall x 3" deep (30.5 cm x 23 cm x 7.5 cm) (not including handles)

WHAT YOU'LL NEED:

Yarn (Medium Weight) 4

[3.5 ounces, 187 yards (100 grams, 171 meters) per skein]:

- ☐ 2 skeins

Crochet Hook

- ☐ Size H (5 mm) **or** size needed for gauge

Notions

- ☐ Craft stabilizer
- ☐ Lining fabric
- ☐ Zipper
- ☐ ¾" (19 mm) Jute cord
- ☐ Yarn needle
- ☐ Sewing needle & matching thread

GAUGE INFORMATION

In pattern (mixed cluster st), 14 sts and 11 rows = 4" (10 cm)

Gauge Swatch: 4¼" wide x 4" high (10.75 cm x 10 cm)

Ch 16.

Work same as Back, page 44, for 11 rows: 15 sts.

Finish off.

STITCH GUIDE

MIXED CLUSTER STITCH

(abbreviated mcs) (uses 3 sts)
YO, insert hook in st indicated, YO and pull up a loop, YO and draw through 2 loops on hook (2 loops on hook), YO, skip **next** st, insert hook in **next** st, YO and pull up a loop (4 loops on hook), YO, insert hook in **same** st, YO and pull up a loop (6 loops on hook), YO and draw through all 6 loops on hook.

BACK

Beginning at bottom, ch 42.

Row 1 (RS)**:** Sc in third ch from hook and in each ch across: 41 sts.

Note: Loop a short piece of yarn around any stitch to mark Row 1 as **right** side.

Row 2: Ch 2, turn; beginning in first st work mcs, ★ ch 1, beginning in same st as previous mcs, work mcs; repeat from ★ across, hdc in top of turning ch.

Row 3: Ch 1, turn; skip first hdc, sc in each st across, working last st in top of turning ch.

Rows 4-24: Repeat Rows 2 and 3, 10 times; then repeat Row 2 once **more**.

Finish off.

FRONT

Work same as Back for 17 rows.

Row 18 (First half)**:** Ch 2, turn; beginning in first st work mcs, ★ ch 1, beginning in same st as previous mcs, work mcs; repeat from ★ 4 times **more**, ch 1; finish off.

Row 18 (Second half)**:** Do **not** turn; skip next 15 sc and join yarn with slip st in next sc; ch 2, beginning in same st as joining, work mcs, ★ ch 1, beginning in same st as previous mcs, work mcs; repeat from ★ 4 times **more** ending last repeat in top of turning ch, hdc in next ch.

Row 19: Ch 1, turn; sc in first 13 sts of Second Half, ch 15, sc in next 13 sts on First Half.

Rows 20-24: Complete same as Back.

SIDE PANEL

Ch 14.

Row 1 (RS)**:** Sc in third ch from hook and in each ch across: 13 sts.

Note: Mark Row 1 as **right** side.

Row 2: Ch 2, turn; beginning in first st work mcs, ★ ch 1, beginning in same st as previous mcs, work mcs; repeat from ★ across, hdc in top of turning ch.

Row 3: Ch 1, turn; skip first hdc, sc in each st across, working last st in top of turning ch.

Rows 4-80: Repeat Rows 2 and 3, 38 times; then repeat Row 2 once **more**.

Finish off.

STRAP (Make 2)

Ch 10.

Row 1 (RS)**:** Sc in third ch from hook and in each ch across: 9 sts.

Note: Mark Row 1 as **right** side.

Row 2: Ch 2, turn; beginning in first st work mcs, ★ ch 1, beginning in same st as previous mcs, work mcs; repeat from ★ across, hdc in top of turning ch.

Row 3: Ch 1, turn; skip first hdc, sc in each st across, working last st in top of turning ch.

Rows 4-49: Repeat Rows 2 and 3, 23 times.

Finish off.

FINISHING

Use finished pieces to cut craft stabilizer and lining fabric.
Sew craft stabilizer in place, being sure to cut out the hole for the zipper created in the front.
Stitch zipper in front opening.
Sew lining fabrics of front and back to side panel lining.
Use working yarn to sew bag front and back to side panel.
Attach lining to top of bag.
Sew cord inside straps. Attach straps to bag using photo as a guide for placement.

Grommet *Bag*

This bag uses a simple construction technique for the bag parts, then ups the game with the addition of large grommets and a ribbon.

INTERMEDIATE

Finished Size: Approximately 11" wide x 9" high x 5" deep (28 cm x 23 cm x 12.5 cm) (not including handles)

WHAT YOU'LL NEED:

Yarn (Super Bulky Weight) SUPER BULKY 6
[7 ounces, 87 yards (200 grams, 80 meters) per ball**]**:
☐ 2 balls

Crochet Hook
☐ Size N/P (10 mm) **or** size needed for gauge

Notions
☐ Craft Stabilizer
☐ Lining fabric
☐ 22" (56 cm) Handles (fabric handles from JoAnn)
☐ Silk scarf or wide ribbon
☐ Grommets (Everything Mary from JoAnn)
☐ Yarn needle
☐ Sewing needle & matching thread

GAUGE INFORMATION
9 sc and 9 rows = 4" (10 cm)
Gauge Swatch: 4" (10 cm) square
Ch 10.
Row 1: Sc in second ch from hook and in each ch across: 9 sc.
Rows 2-9: Ch 1, turn; sc in each sc across.
Finish off.

STITCH GUIDE
INVISIBLE JOIN
Cut yarn and pull through center of last st made. (Do NOT finish off the regular way). Insert hook from **right** to **left** in second st to left and pull yarn through. Insert hook from **right** to **left** in the middle of the last st made (the one you pulled the yarn through initially) and pull yarn down through the middle of this stitch; weave in end.

MAIN PANEL (Make 2)

Beginning at bottom edge, ch 26.

Row 1 (RS)**:** Sc in second ch from hook and in each ch across: 25 sc.

Note: Loop a short piece of yarn around any stitch to mark Row 1 as **right** side.

Row 2: Ch 1, turn; sc in Front Loop Only (FLO) of first sc ***(Fig. 4, page 63)***, ★ sc in Back Loop Only (BLO) of next sc, sc in Front Loop Only (FLO) of next sc; repeat from ★ across.

Rows 3-18: Ch 1, turn; sc in FLO of first sc, ★ sc in BLO of next sc, sc in FLO of next sc; repeat from ★ across.

Row 19: Ch 1, turn; sc in FLO of first sc, sc in BLO of next sc, sc in FLO of next sc, ch 1, skip next sc (grommet opening), sc in FLO of next sc, ★ (sc in BLO of next sc, sc in FLO of next sc) twice, ch 1, skip next sc (grommet opening), sc in FLO of next sc; repeat from ★ 2 times **more**, sc in BLO of next sc, sc in FLO of last sc: 21 sc and 4 ch-1 sps.

Row 20: Ch 1, turn; sc in FLO of first sc, sc in BLO of next sc, sc in FLO of next sc, sc in next ch-1 sp, sc in FLO of next sc, ★ (sc in BLO of next sc, sc in FLO of next sc) twice, sc in next ch-1 sp, sc in FLO of next sc; repeat from ★ 2 times **more**, sc in BLO of next sc, sc in FLO of last sc; finish off: 25 sc.

BASE

Ch 26.

Row 1 (RS)**:** Sc in second ch from hook and in each ch across: 25 sc.

Note: Mark Row 1 as **right** side.

Rows 2-10: Ch 1, turn; sc in FLO of first sc, ★ sc in BLO of next sc, sc in FLO of next sc; repeat from ★ across.

Finish off.

SIDE PANEL (Make 2)

Beginning at bottom, ch 11.

Row 1 (RS)**:** Sc in second ch from hook and in each ch across: 10 sc.

Note: Mark Row 1 as **right** side.

Row 2: Ch 1, turn; sc in FLO of first sc, sc in BLO of next sc, ★ sc in FLO of next sc, sc in BLO of next sc; repeat from ★ across.

Row 3: Ch 1, turn; sc in BLO of first sc, sc in FLO of next sc, ★ sc in BLO of next sc, sc in FLO of next sc; repeat from ★ across.

Rows 4-18: Repeat Rows 2 and 3, 7 times; then repeat Row 2 once **more**.

Row 19: Ch 1, turn; sc in BLO of first sc, (sc in FLO of next sc, sc in BLO of next sc) twice, ch 1, skip next sc (grommet opening), (sc in BLO of next sc, sc in FLO of next sc) twice: 9 sc and one ch-1 sp.

Row 20: Ch 1, turn; sc in FLO of first sc, sc in BLO of next sc, sc in FLO of next sc, sc in BLO of next sc, sc in next ch-1 sp, sc in BLO of next sc, (sc in FLO of next sc, sc in BLO of next sc) twice; finish off: 10 sc.

FINISHING

Use finished pieces to cut craft stabilizer and lining fabric.
Sew craft stabilizer to back of crocheted fabric, making sure to cut holes for grommets.
Use working yarn to sew Main Panels to Side Panels; sew Base to bottom of Panels.
Sew handles in place.
Sew lining pieces together. Sew to bag at top, folding the lining fabric down at the top edge.
Create holes in lining for grommets.
Attach grommets. Weave ribbon through grommets.

Tapestry Drawstring *Backpack*

This bag uses a tapestry design to create interest on a simple drawstring tote. The use of a bag base makes this project a breeze.

■■■□ **INTERMEDIATE**

Finished Size: Approximately 10" wide x 11" tall x 4½" deep (25.5 cm x 28 cm x 11.5 cm)

WHAT YOU'LL NEED:

Yarn (Medium Weight) (4 MEDIUM)

[1.75 ounces, 135 yards (50 grams, 120 meters) per ball**]**:

- ☐ MC (Rust) - 3 balls
- ☐ CC1 (Gold) - 1 ball
- ☐ CC2 (Green) - 1 ball
- ☐ CC3 (Tan) - 1 ball

Crochet Hook

- ☐ Size I (5.5 mm) **or** size needed for gauge

Notions

- ☐ Stitch marker
- ☐ Locking stitch marker
- ☐ Leather bag base
- ☐ 1¼" (32 mm) Nylon strapping - 1 yard (91.5 meters)
- ☐ Lining fabric
- ☐ Yarn needle
- ☐ Sewing needle & matching thread

GAUGE INFORMATION

17 sc and 14 rows/rounds = 4" (10 cm)
Gauge Swatch: 4" (10 cm) square
Ch 18.
Row 1: Sc in second ch from hook and in each ch across: 17 sc.
Rows 2-14: Ch 1, turn; sc in each sc across.
Finish off.

STITCH GUIDE

SINGLE CROCHET 2 TOGETHER
(abbreviated sc2tog)
Pull up a loop in each of next 2 sc, YO and draw through all 3 loops on hook **(counts as one sc)**.

Refer to Tapestry Crochet, page 30, before beginning your Backpack.

The Leather Bag base has 60 holes and the pattern is worked off of this number.

BODY

Rnd 1 (RS)**:** Drawing loops through the holes in the Base, join MC with sc in a side hole ***(see Joining With Sc, page 62)***; sc in each hole around; do not join, place a marker to indicate the beginning of the rnd: 60 sc.

Rnd 2: ★ Sc in next sc, 2 sc in next sc; repeat from ★ around: 90 sc.

Rnds 3-6: Sc in each sc around; drop MC to **wrong** side to carry loosely on back of work.

Rnd 7: With CC2, sc in each sc around.

Rnd 8: (With MC sc in next sc, with CC2 sc in next sc) around; cut MC.

Rnd 9: With CC2, sc in each sc around; cut CC2.

Rnd 10: With CC3, ★ sc2tog, sc in next 43 sc; repeat from ★ once **more**: 88 sc.

Rnds 11-35: Follow chart; at end of Rnd 35, cut all colors.

CHART

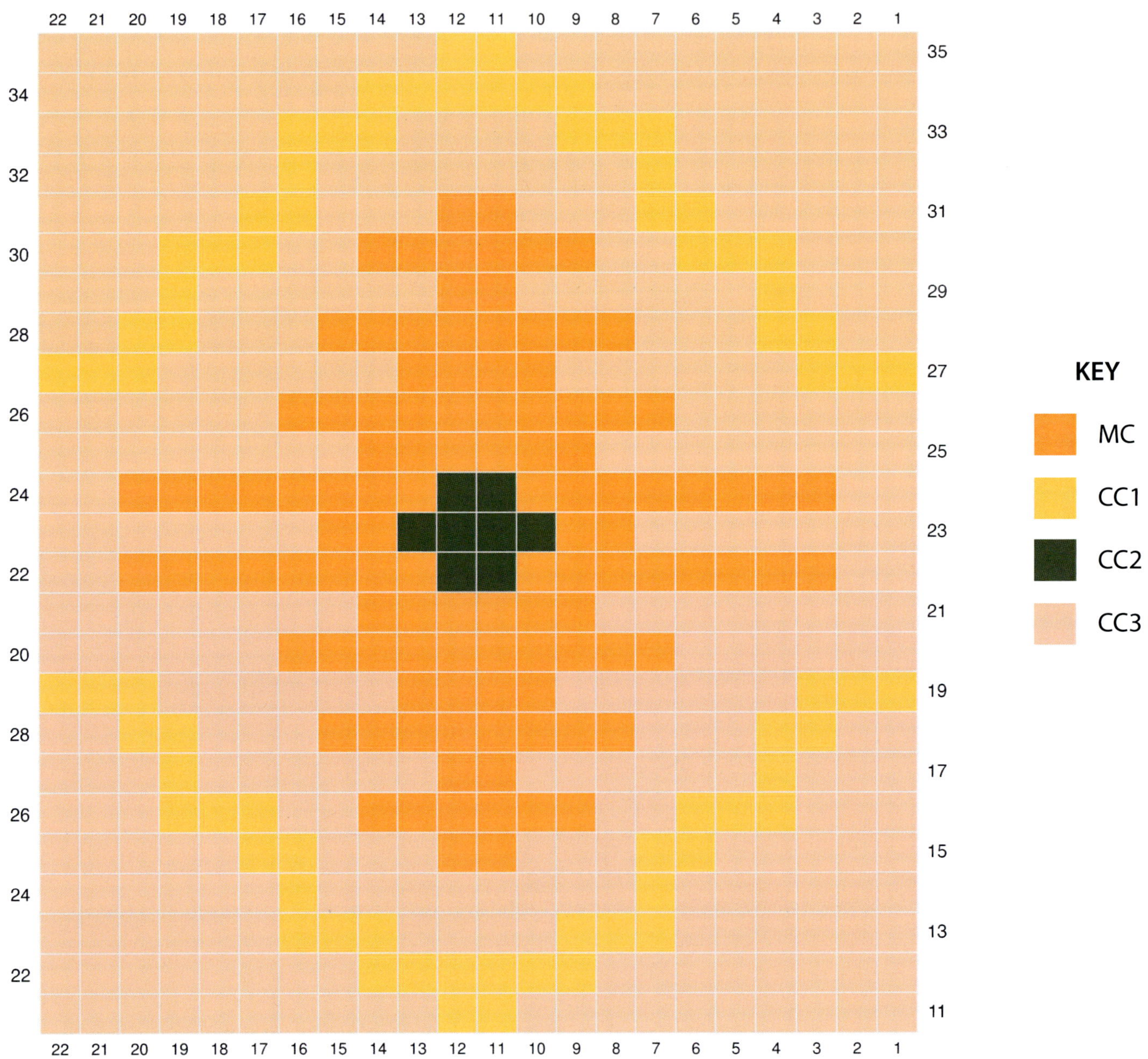

Rnd 36: With CC2, sc in each sc around.

Rnd 37: (With MC sc in next sc, with CC2 sc in next sc) around; drop MC.

Rnd 38: With CC2, sc in each sc around; cut CC2.

Rnds 39-42: With MC, sc in each sc around.

Mark center front st with locking st marker.

Rnd 43: Sc in each sc to marked st, ch 1, skip marked st, sc in each sc around.

Rnds 44-49: Sc in each st around.

Finish off.

STRAP
Cut 2 pieces of nylon strapping, each 18" (45.5 cm) long.

With MC, ch 13.

Row 1: Sc in second ch from hook and in each ch across: 12 sc.

Row 2: Ch, 1 turn; sc in each sc across.

Repeat Row 2 until piece measures 18" (45.5 cm) long.

Finish off leaving a long end for sewing.

Place nylon strap inside crocheted strip and fold in half; sew seam.

FINISHING
Use one 50" (127 cm) strand of **each** contrasting color to create drawstring.
Braid three strands together.
With drawstring inside, fold down top of bag to **wrong** side, matching Row 39 to Row 49. Pull drawstring ends through ch-1 sp at marker.
Sew Row 39 to Row 49.
Sew straps in place as shown in photos.
Use finished bag to create lining.
Stitch lining side seam and stitch to bottom.
Attach inside of bag to Row 39.

Arabel Cabled *Tote*

This tote uses a purchased bag base and top combined with a super bulky yarn for a super quick project. The waistcoat stitch gives it a knit look and the cable adds visual interest.

INTERMEDIATE

Finished Size: Approximately 12" wide x 12" tall x 4" deep (30.5 cm x 30.5 cm x 10 cm) (not including handle)

WHAT YOU'LL NEED:

Yarn (Super Bulky Weight)

SUPER BULKY 6

[3.5 ounces, 52 yards (100 grams, 48 meters) per ball]:

- ☐ 3 balls

Crochet Hooks

- ☐ Size H (5 mm) **and**
- ☐ Size N/P (10 mm)
  or sizes needed for gauge

Notions

- ☐ Stitch marker
- ☐ Craft stabilizer
- ☐ Lining fabric
- ☐ Knitter's Pride Sew-On Bag Kit
- ☐ Yarn needle
- ☐ Sewing needle & matching thread

GAUGE INFORMATION

In pattern (waistcoat st),
8 sts and 10 rows/rounds = 4" (10 cm)

Gauge Swatch: 4" (10 cm) square with larger size hook, ch 9.

Row 1: Sc in second ch from hook and in each ch across: 8 sc.

Rows 2-10: Ch 1, turn; work in wst in each st across.

Finish off.

NOTES

The base of the Knitter's Pride Bag Kit has 52 holes and the pattern is worked off of this number. The top of the Knitter's Pride Kit has 40 holes. Do **not** join or turn at the end of the round. The bag is worked continually in rounds.

STITCH GUIDE

SINGLE CROCHET 2 TOGETHER

Pull up a loop in each of next 2 sts (as in waistcoat stitch), YO and draw through all 3 loops on hook.

FRONT POST DOUBLE CROCHET *(abbreviated FPdc)*

YO, insert hook from **front** to **back** around post of st indicated ***(Fig. 6, page 62)***, YO and pull up a loop (3 loops on hook), (YO and draw through 2 loops on hook) twice. Skip st **behind** FPdc.

FRONT POST TREBLE CROCHET *(abbreviated FPtr)*

YO twice, insert hook from **front** to **back** around post of st indicated ***(Fig. 6, page 62)***, YO and pull up a loop (4 loops on hook), (YO and draw through 2 loops on hook) 3 times. Skip st **behind** FPtr.

WAISTCOAT STITCH *(abbreviated wst)*

Work same as a sc inserting hook between the "legs" of the st ***(Fig. A)***.

Fig. A

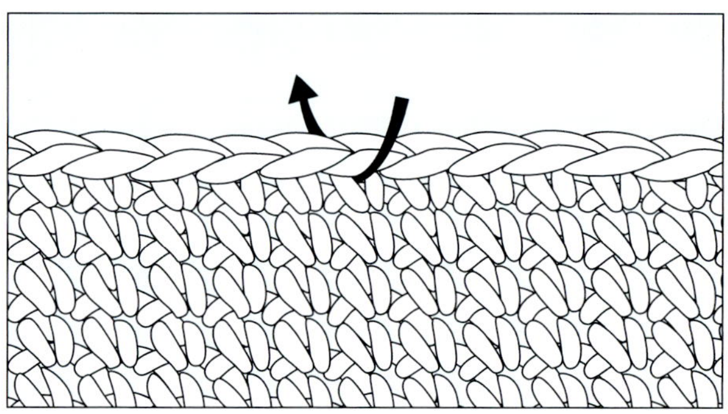

BODY

Foundation Rnd (RS)**:** With larger size hook, place slip knot on hook. With **right** side of Base facing, pull up a loop in any hole using smaller size hook, place this loop on larger hook, YO and draw through both loops on larger hook **(sc completed)**, ★ pull up a loop in next hole using smaller size hook, place this loop on larger hook, YO and draw through both loops on larger hook; repeat from ★ around; do **not** join, place a marker to indicated the beginning of the rnd ***(see Markers, page 60)***: 52 sc.

Rnd 1: Work next 10 sts in wst, dc in next 6 sts, work next 20 sts in wst, dc in next 6 sts, work next 10 sts in wst.

Rnd 2: Work next 10 sts in wst, † skip next 2 sts, work FPtr around each of next 2 sts, working in **front** of FPtr just made, work FPtr around each of 2 skipped sts, work FPdc around each of next 2 sts †, work next 20 sts in wst, repeat from † to † once, work next 10 sts in wst.

Rnd 3: Work next 10 sts in wst, work FPdc around each of next 6 sts, work next 20 sts in wst, work FPdc around each of next 6 sts, work next 10 sts in wst.

Rnd 4: Work next 10 sts in wst, † work FPdc around each of next 2 sts, skip next 2 sts, work FPtr around each of next 2 sts, working in **front** of FPtr just made, work FPtr around each of 2 skipped sts †, work next 20 sts in wst, repeat from † to † once, work next 10 sts in wst.

Rnd 5: Work next 10 sts in wst, work FPdc around each of next 6 sts, work next 20 sts in wst, work FPdc around each of next 6 sts, work next 10 sts in wst.

Rnds 6-16: Repeat Rnds 2-5 twice, then repeat Rnds 2-4 once **more**.

Rnd 17: ★ (Sc2tog in wst) twice, work next 6 sts in wst, sc2tog in wst, work next 6 sts in wst; repeat from ★ once **more**, sc2tog in wst, work next 6 sts in wst, sc2tog in wst, work next 6 sts in wst; finish off leaving a long end for sewing Body to Top: 44 sts.

With long end, sew Top to crocheted fabric, working 2 times through each hole as seen in photo.

FINISHING

Use finished pieces to cut craft stabilizer and lining fabric.
Sew craft stabilizer to back of crocheted fabric.
Sew lining pieces together. Sew to bag at top, directly underneath bag top.

General *Instructions*

ABBREVIATIONS

BLO	back loop only
CC	Contrasting Color
ch(s)	chain(s)
cm	centimeters
dc	double crochet(s)
FLO	front loop only
FPdc	Front Post double crochet(s)
FPtr	Front Post treble crochet(s)
FPtr2tog	Front Post treble crochet 2 together
hdc	half double crochet(s)
hdc2tog	half double crochet 2 together
mbs	modified bean stitch(s)
mbs2tog	modified bean stitch 2 together
MC	Main Color
mcs	mixed cluster stitch(es)
mm	millimeters
Rnd(s)	round(s)
RS	right side
sc	single crochet(s)
sc2tog	single crochet 2 together
sc3tog	single crochet 3 together
sp(s)	space(s)
st(s)	stitch(es)
tog	together
wst	waistcoat stitch
YO	yarn over

SYMBOLS & TERMS

★ — work instructions following ★ as many **more** times as indicated in addition to the first time.

† to † — work all instructions from first † to second † **as many** times as specified.

( ) or **[ ]** — work enclosed instructions **as many** times as specified by the number immediately following **or** work all enclosed instruction in the stitch or space indicated **or** contains explanatory remarks.

colon (:) — the number(s) given after a colon at the end of a row or round denote(s) the number of stitches or spaces you should have on that row or round.

CROCHET TERMINOLOGY		
UNITED STATES		INTERNATIONAL
slip stitch (slip st)	=	single crochet (sc)
single crochet (sc)	=	double crochet (dc)
half double crochet (hdc)	=	half treble crochet (htr)
double crochet (dc)	=	treble crochet (tr)
treble crochet (tr)	=	double treble crochet (dtr)
double treble crochet (dtr)	=	triple treble crochet (ttr)
triple treble crochet (tr tr)	=	quadruple treble crochet (qtr)
skip	=	miss

GAUGE

Exact gauge in **essential** for proper size. Before beginning your project, make the sample swatch given in the individual instructions in the yarn and hook specified. After completing the swatch, measure it, counting your stitches and rows or rounds carefully. If your swatch is larger or smaller than specified, **make another, changing hook size to get the correct gauge**. Keep trying until you find the size hook that will give you the specified gauge.

MARKERS

Markers are used to help distinuish the beginning of each round being worked. Place a 2" (5 cm) scrap piece of yarn before the first stitch of each round, moving marker after each round is complete.

Yarn Weight Symbol & Names	LACE 0	SUPER FINE 1	FINE 2	LIGHT 3	MEDIUM 4	BULKY 5	SUPER BULKY 6	JUMBO 7
Type of Yarns in Category	Fingering, size 10 crochet thread	Sock, Fingering, Baby	Sport, Baby	DK, Light Worsted	Worsted, Afghan, Aran	Chunky, Craft, Rug	Super Bulky, Roving	Jumbo, Roving
Crochet Gauge* Ranges in Single Crochet to 4" (10 cm)	32-42 sts**	21-32 sts	16-20 sts	12-17 sts	11-14 sts	8-11 sts	6-9 sts	5 sts and fewer
Advised Hook Size Range	Steel*** 6 to 8, Regular hook B-1	B-1 to E-4	E-4 to 7	7 to I-9	I-9 to K-10½	K-10½ to M/N-13	M/N-13 to Q	Q and larger

*GUIDELINES ONLY: The chart above reflects the most commonly used gauges and hook sizes for specific yarn categories.

** Lace weight yarns are usually crocheted with larger hooks to create lacy openwork patterns. Accordingly, a gauge range is difficult to determine. Always follow the gauge stated in your pattern.

*** Steel crochet hooks are sized differently from regular hooks–the higher the number, the smaller the hook, which is the reverse of regular hook sizing.

BASIC	Projects using basic stitches. May include basic increases and decreases.
EASY	Projects may include simple stitch patterns, color work, and/or shaping.
INTERMEDIATE	Projects may include involved stitch patterns, color work, and/or shaping.
COMPLEX	Projects may include complex stitch patterns, color work, and/or shaping using a variety of techniques and stitches simultaneously.

CROCHET HOOKS

U.S.	B-1	C-2	D-3	E-4	F-5	G-6	7	H-8	I-9	J-10	K-10½	L-11	M/N-13	N/P-15	P/Q	Q	S
Metric - mm	2.25	2.75	3.25	3.5	3.75	4	4.5	5	5.5	6	6.5	8	9	10	15	16	19

JOINING WITH SC

When instructed to join with sc, begin with a slip knot on the hook. Insert the hook in the stitch indicated, YO and pull up a loop, YO and draw through both loops on hook.

ADJUSTABLE LOOP

Wind the yarn around two fingers to form a ring ***(Fig. 1a)***, slide the yarn off your fingers and grasp the strands at the top of the ring ***(Fig. 1b)***. Insert the hook from **front** to **back** into the ring, YO and pull up a loop, YO and draw through the loop on hook to lock the ring ***(Fig. 1c)***. Working around both strands, work stitches in the ring as specified, then pull the yarn end to close ***(Fig. 1d)***.

Fig. 1a

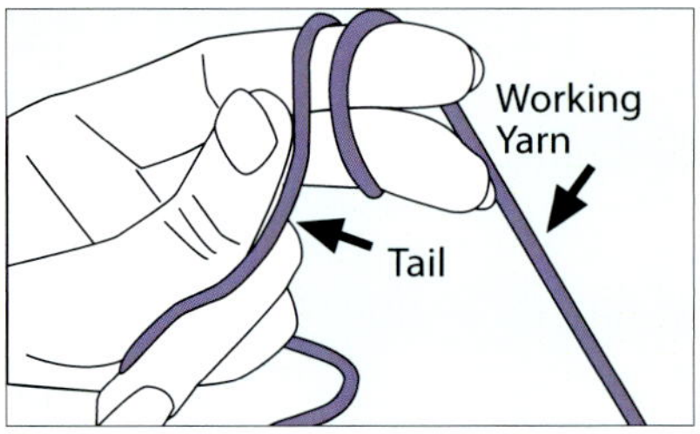

Fig. 1c

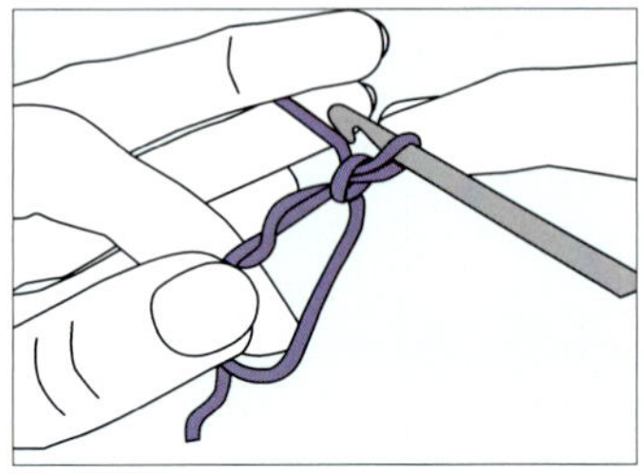

Fig. 1b

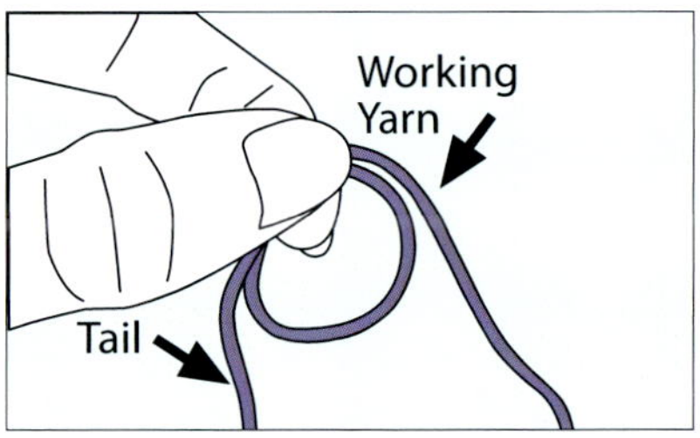

Fig. 1d

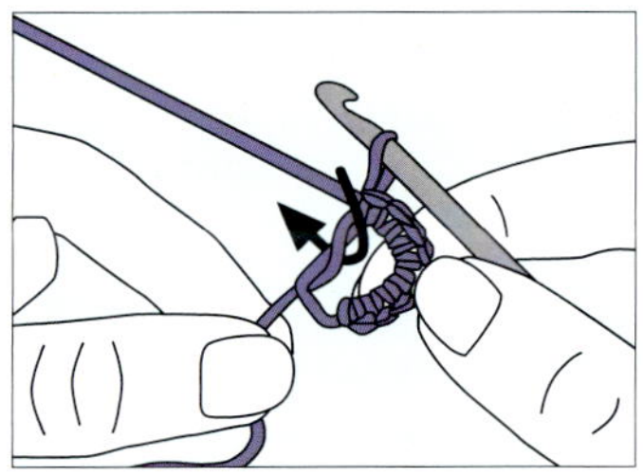

BACK RIDGE

Work only in loops indicated by arrows ***(Fig. 2)***.

Fig. 2

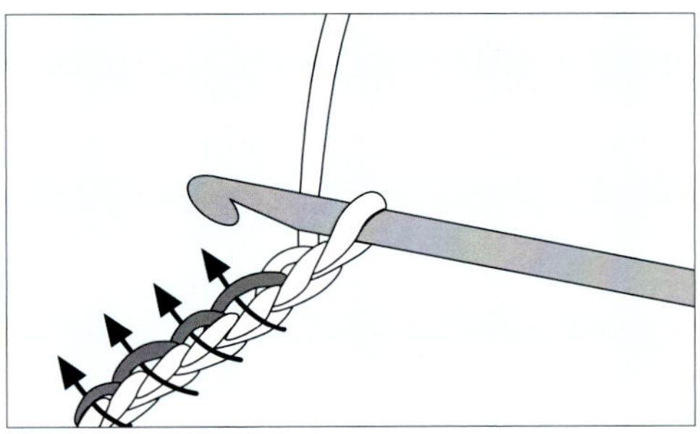

POST STITCH

Insert hook around post of stitch indicated, working in direction of arrow ***(Fig. 6)***.

Fig. 6

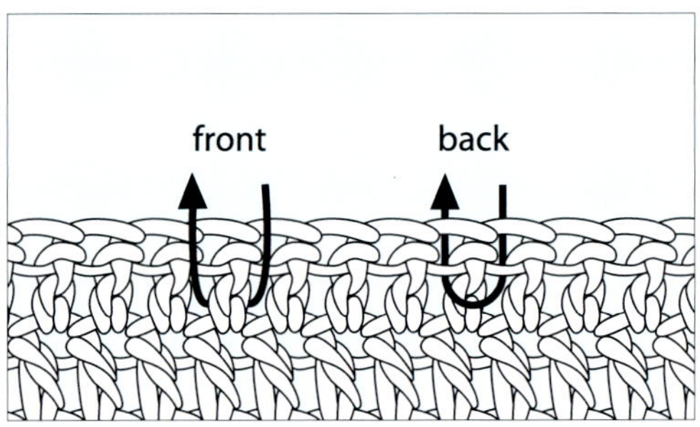

FREE LOOPS OF A CHAIN

When instructed to work in free loops of a chain, work in loop(s) indicated by arrow ***(Figs. 3a & b)***.

Fig. 3a

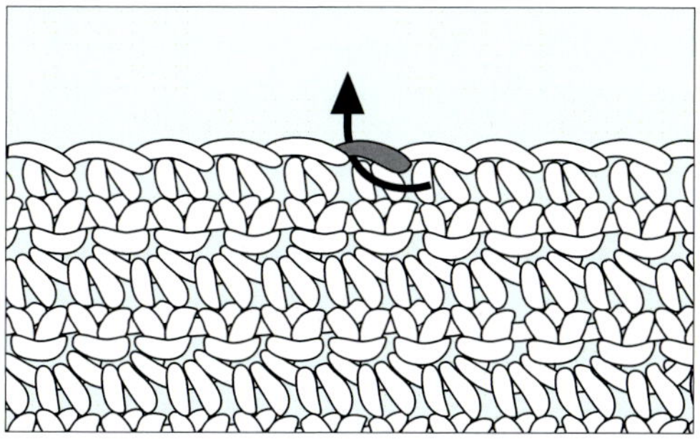

Fig. 3b

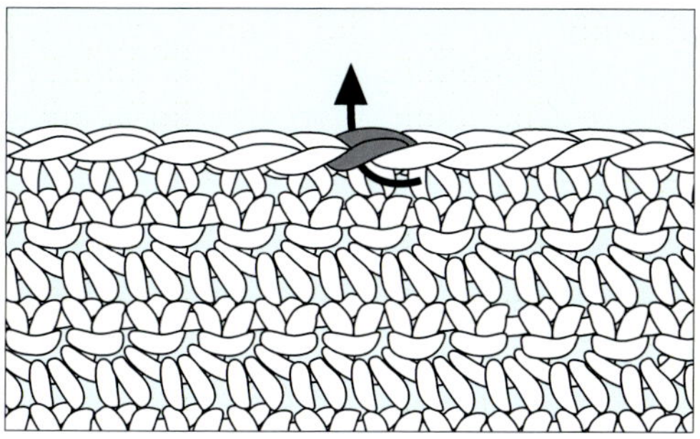

BACK OR FRONT LOOP ONLY

Work only in loop(s) indicated by arrow ***(Fig. 4)***.

Fig. 4

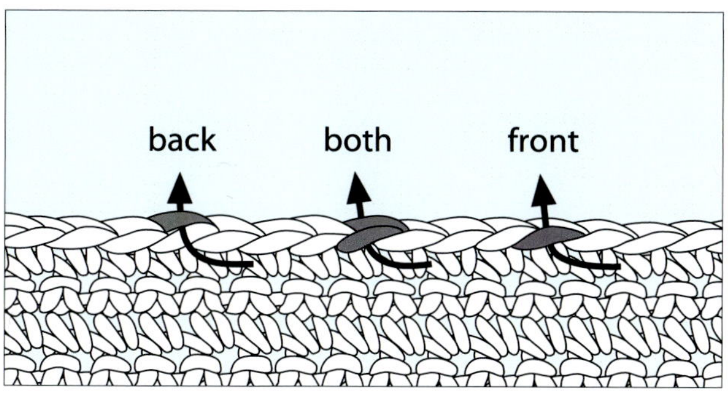

CHANGING COLORS

To change colors while joining with a slip st, drop working yarn, insert hook in st indicated, hook new color yarn and draw through the st and the loop on the hook ***(Fig. 5a)***.

Fig. 5a

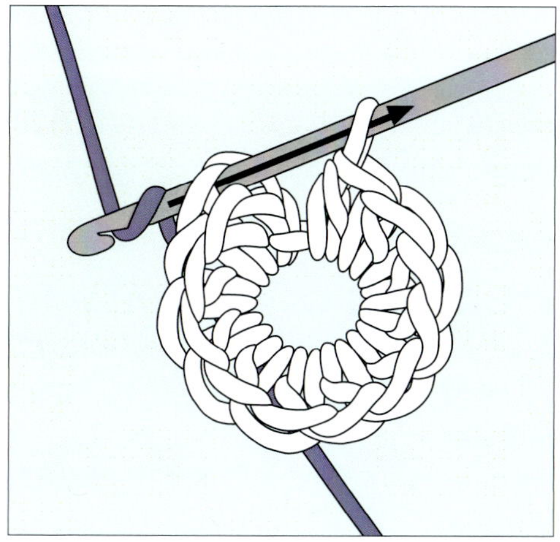

To change color at the end of the row, work last stitch to within one step of completion, drop old color, with new color, YO and draw through all loops on hook ***(Fig. 5b)***.

Fig. 5b

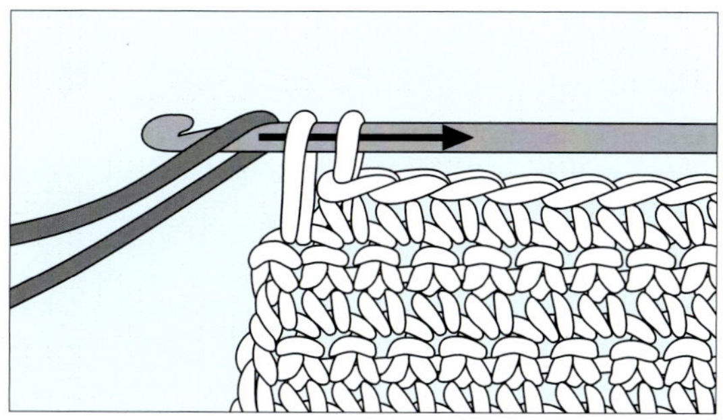

YARN INFORMATION

The Handbags in this book were made using a variety of yarns. Any brand of the specified weight of yarn may be used. It is best to refer to the yardage/meters when determining how many balls, skeins or hanks to purchase. Remember, to achieve the same look, it is the weight of yarn that is important, not the brand of yarn.

For your convenience, listed below are the specific yarns used to create our photography models. Because yarn manufacturers make frequent changes to their product lines, you may sometimes find it necessary to use a substitute yarn or to search for the discontinued product at alternate suppliers (locally or online).

DIAMOND COIN PURSE
LB Collection® Merino Camel
#110 Navy

DOUBLE ZIPPER TRAVEL BAG
Sugarbush Crisp
MC (Gray) - #2019 Lead
CC1 (Black) - #2020 Zinc
CC2 (Blue/Gray) -
#2022 Bonavista Blue
CC3 (Blue) - #2015 French Blue

PUFF STITCH CLUTCH
LB Collection® Hand Dyed Silk
#203 Sapphire

TOTE WITH ZIPPER POCKET
Red Heart® Colorscapes™
#6342 Montreal

GROMMET BAG
LB Collection® Fifty Fifty
#153 Black

TAPESTRY DRAWSTRING BACKPACK
LB Collection® Chainette
MC (Rust) - #186 Amber
CC1 (Gold) - #159 Mustard
CC2 (Green) - #174 Olive
CC3 (Tan) - #123 Beige

ARABEL CABLED TOTE
Sugarbush Chill
#1014 Alpine

We have made every effort to ensure that these instructions are accurate and complete. We cannot, however, be responsible for human error, typographical mistakes, or variations in individual work.

Production Team: Project Manager/Technical Editor - Linda A. Daley; Graphic Artists - Katie Cooper-Bussell & Mark Hawkins; Photo Stylist - Lori Wenger; and Photographer - Jason Masters.

Made in U.S.A.